POEMS
NEW AND SELECTED

Other Books in Print by James Laughlin

Poetry

SELECTED POEMS 1935–1985
(*City Lights*)

THE OWL OF MINERVA
(*Copper Canyon Press*)

THE BIRD OF ENDLESS TIME
(*Copper Canyon Press*)

COLLECTED POEMS, 1938–1992
(*Moyer Bell Limited*)

THE MAN IN THE WALL
(*New Directions*)

HEART ISLAND
(*Turkey Press*)

REMEMBERING WILLIAM CARLOS WILLIAMS
(*New Directions*)

THE COUNTRY ROAD
(*Zoland Books*)

PHANTOMS
(*Aperture Books*)

THE SECRET ROOM
(*New Directions*)

THE LOVE POEMS
(*New Directions*)

Prose

POUND AS WUZ
(*Graywolf*)

RANDOM ESSAYS
(*Moyer Bell Limited*)

ANGELICA
(*The Grenfell Press*)

Selected Letters Series

WILLIAM CARLOS WILLIAMS & JAMES LAUGHLIN
KENNETH REXROTH & JAMES LAUGHLIN
EZRA POUND & JAMES LAUGHLIN
HENRY MILLER & JAMES LAUGHLIN
THOMAS MERTON & JAMES LAUGHLIN
(*W.W. Norton & Company*)

JAMES LAUGHLIN

POEMS
NEW AND SELECTED

INTRODUCTION BY
CHARLES TOMLINSON

A NEW DIRECTIONS BOOK

The poems "I Cannot Separate Her" and "Lost Brains" originally appeared in *The New Yorker,* "Nunc Dimittis" in *Double Take,* "Funerals" and "Illness" in *Grand Street,* and "An Honest Heart . . . A Knowing Hand" in *Agni.*

The epigraph on page vii, "Write on My Tomb," was originally published in James Laughlin's *Stolen & Contaminated Poems* (1985).

Most of the poems in this volume were selected from the following books by James Laughlin: *Some Natural Things* (1945), *A Small Book of Poems* (1947), *The Wild Anemone* (1957), *In Another Country* (1978), *Stolen & Contaminated Poems* (1985), *Selected Poems 1935–1985* (1986), *The Owl of Minerva* (1987), *The Bird of Endless Time* (1989), *The Man in the Wall* (1993), *The Collected Poems of James Laughlin* (1994), *Heart Island & Other Epigrams* (1995), *The Country Road* (1995), and *The Secret Room* (1996). For details, see below, p. 291.

Manufactured in the United States of America
New Directions Books are printed on acid-free paper.
First published as New Directions Paperbook 857 in 1998
Published simultaneously in Canada by Penguin Books
Canada Limited

Library of Congress Cataloging-in-Publication Data
Laughlin, James, 1914–1997
   [Poems. Selections]
   Poems, new and selected/James Laughlin; introduction by Charles
Tomlinson.
      p. cm.
   Includes index.
   ISBN 0–8112–1375–7 (pbk.: alk. paper)
   I. Title.
PS3523.A8245A6   1998
811'.54—dc21   97–52320
                                                  CIP

New Directions Books are published for James Laughlin
by New Directions Publishing Corporation,
80 Eighth Avenue, New York 10011

for

GERTRUDE

WRITE ON MY TOMB

that all I learned in books
and from the muses I've ta-

ken with me but my rich pos-
sessions I have left behind.

CONTENTS

FOREWORD

Many of the writings in this book should be called verse rather than poetry. Poetry is an exalted, almost mystical writing in its nature. Poetry works with devices such as metaphor and verbal decoration. This writer seldom aspires to such high levels of expression. His writings are most often the statement of facts as he has discerned them. Many are reports on perceived feelings, his own and those of others; or a placing with imagination; or recollections from reading of matters with which classical writers were concerned. There is a minimum of decoration.

The writer's intention is summarized in the passage of one of his verses which states:

SOME PEOPLE THINK

that poetry should be a–
dorned or complicated. I'm

not so sure. I think I'll
take the simple statement

in plain speech compress–
ed to brevity. I think that

will do all I want to do.

The Greek origin of the term epigram is a scratching on stone. The most pleasing of these verses aspire to live up to that definition. Many fail, but a few succeed.

JAMES LAUGHLIN

INTRODUCTION

James Laughlin's poetry comes mainly in two sizes, short-line poems and long-line poems, and the table of contents here insists on that division. He began by writing in short lines and, of course, he has frequently returned to that form. These poems seem to me to belong at the center of his achievement. Their hold on the exact phrase, intonation, or cadence also makes possible, when he comes to write long-line poems, a flowing distinctiveness and clarity, where many another poet might sound merely diffuse. There is no Whitmanian afflatus: what we hear is the tone of the speaking voice modulated as between friends, the diction nicely adjusted to conveying the matter in hand without overemphasis.

The first poem I ever read by Laughlin happened to be of the short-line variety. Its title was "Above the City." I found it quoted whole by Marianne Moore in an essay called "Humility, Concentration, and Gusto" in her *Predilections*, which I acquired in 1956. At first the poem puzzled me, but rapidly puzzlement turned to delight. There seemed to be two patterns at work, the visual and the oral, each refusing to become reconciled with the other without negotiation and without the reader's active cooperation:

> You know our office on the 18th
> floor of the Salmon Tower looks
> right out on the
>
> Empire State and it just happened
> we were there finishing up some
> late invoices on
>
> a new book that Saturday morning
> when a bomber roared through the
> mist and crashed

> flames poured from the windows
> into the drifting clouds and sirens
> screamed down in
>
> the streets below. . . .

And so it goes unstoppably on, until guided into its coda by three deft but unobtrusive internal rhymes—"realized," "surprised," "eyes"—one in each of the three concluding stanzas. One sees why Marianne Moore was taken by this poem, she whose visual arrangement of her verse so delighted in antagonizing eye and voice. She even went as far as to reorder the last two stanzas and wrote to Laughlin, "Can you condone it?" "I could indeed," the poet gallantly responded when he reprinted "Above the City." Yet one is relieved that he also retained the poem in its original form where the last stanza violates the line count of those preceding, but has more verbal muscularity than Miss Moore's—despite its extra line, which is empowered, in Doctor Johnson's phrase, with "more weight than bulk." Indeed, fundamentally the relation of eye to ear in Laughlin stands far nearer to William Carlos Williams than to Miss Moore. The latter is more interested in arranging her words as if they were patternings on some kind of sampler, elegantly displayed, but not invariably aiming for that precarious unity where the seen and the heard both challenge and reinforce each other, until it is the ear that becomes the final arbiter and measure. In Laughlin one sees the closeness to Williams' playing off the two elements against each other, of (as he says) "poem against metric." Williams unfortunately has a weakness for terminology that sometimes renders ambiguous what he is saying. In "poem against metric" here "metric" seems to gesture toward the way words lie visually on the page and not to the countable recurrence of a beat. This he also sees as a partnership between the oral or "verbal invention" and visual layout. "The poem is here, but the metric is *here*," as Williams writes to one correspondent, "and they go along side by side—the verbal invention and the purely metrical invention—go along arm in arm, looking for a place where they can embrace."

In first reading "Above the City," I liked all the brisk work the eye was called on to do, and I enjoyed that first real shock, the enjambement or stanzaic leap to the famous skyscraper that appears in stanza two. At the same time you heard the speaking voice pulling against stanzaic layout. I could not have known then—long before the publication of Hugh Witemeyer's edition of the correspondence of the two poets—that Laughlin and Williams had been discussing the matter with each other in the late thirties. "Damn the bastards," wrote Williams, "for saying that you can't mix auditory and visual standards in poetry. . . . What they . . . don't know, is that an auditory quality, a NEW auditory quality, underlines and determines the visual quality which they object to." Laughlin himself had been speaking about "the tension . . . between the strictly artificial visual pattern and the strictly natural spoken rhythms," in opposition to his Harvard associates, who disputed this aspect of his poetry.

The earliest of Laughlin's books that I have in my possession bears the date of 1945. It was poems from this collection, *Some Natural Things,* which opened *The Collected Poems* of 1994. Between these two dates you might imagine a good deal of fame as a poet would have come his way. Yet look into any of the anthologies—into, say, the benchmark *Norton Anthology of Modern Poetry*—and you can be sure of not finding Laughlin there. The same is true of literary histories—*The Columbia History of American Poetry,* for example: silence. As a famous publisher, you might think he would be regarded as a phenomenon, a publisher who writes excellent verse. One of the blurbs on the 1994 *Collected Poems* says, "Here is America's great popular poet, if only the bastards read poetry." Perhaps one day, when people tire of all those phoney novels, he will be. But not yet.

Over thirty years ago, I asked Henry Rago, the last of the great editors of *Poetry (Chicago),* why one could trace so few notices of Laughlin's books. "Because," said Rago, "he never avails himself of the system of promotion—he even refrains from sending out review copies." So perhaps Laughlin's own modesty is partly to blame? Clearly he had dubious feelings about being his own publisher and apologizes to and for himself in "The Publisher to the Poet":

> Right hand blush never
> for left handed brother
>
> action and thought are
> children of one mother

Laughlin's career as a writer began with Latin and Greek at Choate school. Catullus has always been one of his touchstones. In the notes to *The Collected Poems* (called typically "Not-Notes") he tells us of the next step: "After a boring freshman year at Harvard I took off for Europe and enrolled in Pound's Ezuversity at Rapallo. He was, by all odds, my greatest professor . . . and my education continued for thirty years after I became his publisher." "Ezra," a recent poem of some length (and an earlier version of "Some Memories of E.P."), charts this formative relationship:

> You said I was
> Such a terrible poet, I'd better
> Do something useful and become
> A publisher, a profession which
> You inferred required no talent
> And only limited intelligence.

One of the suggestions made by Pound for this publishing venture was the work of his friend—and soon to become Laughlin's friend—William Carlos Williams. Williams was just the man Laughlin needed to know and read. More, perhaps, even than Pound, it is the stylistic influence of Williams—with a dash of Cummings in the punctuation or lack of it—that enabled Laughlin to develop his own style. Its form—before he went in for longer lines as the imaginary poet Hiram Handspring—was dictated by the typewriter: "The rule is that in a couplet any second line has to be within two typewriter spaces of the line preceding it." The result is a breaking up of those curious things words and sentences and a pleasurable dislocation between what one sees and the cadence of what one reads—you are not meant to pause at the end of every line, as in the verse of Robert Creeley any more than in Marianne Moore's syllabics:

> You know that comical
> puppy has grown up in-
>
> to a marvelous hunting
> dog he's in the woods
>
> all day and brings out
> rabbits by the dozen

but the funny thing is
he never hurts them he

doesn't even bite them
just carries them home

in his mouth & leaves
them on the porch for

us   poor little things
at first they're much

too scared to move but
in a little while they

shake themselves & hop
away to the woods again

It is out of such domestic incidents and the pleasures and pains of love and of family life that Laughlin creates many of his best poems. He has, of late, written of the suicide of his son Robert and the death of his wife Ann. These are unusually harrowing incidents for Laughlin (he writes about them with never a false note), yet it is often the inevitable painful collisions of family relationships, our violations of one another, that give substance to his poems. Laughlin insists that he writes "light verse," but it is not of the Odgen Nash kind. The lightness betokens a sensitivity in handling deceptively simple, but tricky subjects. The head in "Step on His Head" is only a bobbing shadow jumped on by his children, but the incident is fraught with pain to come:

now I duck my head so they'll
miss when they jump & they screech

with delight and I moan oh you're
hurting you're hurting me stop and
they jump all the harder. . . .

The crucial poem of Williams for Laughlin in helping him towards his characteristic style was the former's "The Catholic Bells" with its own dislocations:

> . . . ring for the lame
>
> young man in black with
> gaunt cheeks and wearing a
> Derby hat, who is hurrying
> to 11 o'clock Mass (the
>
> grapes still hanging to
> the vines along the nearby
> Concordia Halle like broken
> teeth in the head of an
>
> old man). . . .

It was after reading this that Laughlin wrote "Easter in Pittsburgh," his longest poem to date, and one in which the subject matter of the family—the uncle who preaches and drinks, the sacked maid and governess, the strike in Pittsburgh and tear gas at the steel mill—all comes into focus and availability. Lowell in *Life Studies* seems to have learned something from Laughlin's poem and also from his "The Swarming Bees" (on Uncle Willy, another drinking relation). Lowell, writing about William Carlos Williams and also paying tribute to "The Catholic Bells," says of Laughlin at Harvard: "our only strong and avant-garde man was James Laughlin. . . . He knew the great, and he himself wrote deliberately flat descriptive and anecdotal poems. We were sarcastic about them, but they made us feel secretly that we didn't know what was up in poetry." Williams' two poems on his own parents, "Adam" and "Eve" of 1936, appeared to have given food for thought to both Lowell and Laughlin.

It was in "Easter in Pittsburgh" that Laughlin most energetically carried forward the dramatic qualities that Williams had discovered in the cadences of the natural speaking voice when he had written "The Catholic Bells." This was an historic moment. It seemed to Williams that Laughlin had taken what he himself had done and extended its possibilities. The realization and mark of understanding between the older poet and the younger show significantly in a letter Williams wrote to Laughlin in 1939: "The Easter in Pittsburgh is a milestone. That's a noteworthy poem, a revolutionary poem in more ways than one. I'm thinking of the form of it. . . . It gains dignity at your hands, it reveals the possibilities in the form, possibilities for the long sought dramatic unit of speech, of composition that can go anywhere it wants to." Williams then confesses, "The one thing that has disturbed me at times is that my studies and labors in the form of verse have not shown a quality susceptible of further development. I've had a few imitators but no one, till now, who seemed to be able to take what I've done and step it up to the next level."

The marks of Laughlin's poetry are its humanity and its variety of both themes and idiom. Besides the poems in English, there are those in "(American) French," at least one in ski-slopes German, and those that use Italian. The most beautiful of these last form a sequence which recounts a love affair between the young poet and an Italian girl, "In Another Country":

> she called vieni qua splashing her
> arms in the clear green water vieni
> subito and so I followed her swim-
> ming around a point of rock to the
>
> next cove vieni qua non hai paura
> and she slipped like an eel beneath
> the surface down through the sunken
> entrance to a hidden grotto where
>
> the light was soft and green on fine-
> grained sand è bello no? . . .

A number of the poems have this "light that never was on sea or land" ("è strano questa luce com' un / altro mondo"), but the majority take place in the world of common experience, as effortlessly unstrained as Williams' poem on the plums in the icebox.

One values these poems for their use of a wide and unexpected subject matter—the small boy, for instance, who fashions cardboard hatchets, bloodstains their blades with red crayon, and lays them affectionately on his father's work desk. "Anything," as Williams stated, "is

good material for poetry. Anything. I've said it time and time again."
Laughlin evidently agrees with this contention. Yet there is more to
the end result than the sheer randomness of merely "some natural
things" (the title of one of his books). In describing his way of writ-
ing ("Technical Notes"), Laughlin explains that he prefers, as against
using poetic diction,

> to build with plain brown bricks
> of common talk American talk then
> set 1 Roman stone
>
> among them for a key

This keystone and sense of cumulative architecture in these carefully
assembled structures represent the conversion of everyday matter into
the matter of art. "With me a poem," says Laughlin,

> is finally just
> a natural thing

And yet, as Guy Davenport has put it, in "a neat oblong of phrases,
squared away on the page, each line [is] a little event in itself." These
events impress us for the shapeliness of their appearance, their having
been "squared" into inevitability and also possessing a keystone. What
we listen to is the natural speech with which Laughlin begins now
brought to an aesthetic focus by the heard measure of the poems.
These are the products of many decades in which "the shaping spirit
of the imagination" combines its forces with those of nature.

CHARLES TOMLINSON

BOOK I

NEW POEMS

PATTERNS

I'm past eighty now and as I sit down
at the typewriter to slip a fresh
sheet of paper under the roller
I see again that the raised veins
of old age make a pattern on
the back of my left hand.
What kind of pattern is it?

It's nothing recognizable in nature,
it's not the leaf from a tree;
nothing like that. It must be
a message, and I know what the message
is; that, to put it in a poetic way,
there will soon be a knocking
at the door.

But for the interim what does
the writing in the pattern say?
Is it the inscription on the stone
that is the lintel of the temple
of the oracle at Delphi? Does it
spell out the prophecy of Tiresias
that Odysseus will live to return
to Ithaca and the arms of Penelope?
Is it the scrawl that Ariadne
made on the beach of Naxos when
she was waiting for Theseus to return?

THE ILLUSION

Looking through my new book of poems
that has just come from the bindery
I see that many lines of black type are
printed on white paper.
So what? This is nothing exceptional.
Many thousands of versifiers have written
before me, and as many more will follow me
if the world lasts.
So what? Here today and gone tomorrow.
The illusion of poetry.

THE SPY

I'm convinced from a few words
she let drop that while she lay
beside me in bed, I asleep
and she awake, she began to spy
on my dreams. I must find out
what she was after.

Was she trying to find out
if I still loved her? I do,
very much. Is some jealousy
at work? Did I talk to Jennifer
too much at the party? (Jennifer
can be very amusing.)

Does she suspect that as much
as I show my love for her
I'm really some kind of monster
that doesn't belong in the human race?

How should I trap the beautiful
intruder? Should I perhaps
pretend to talk in my sleep
and make up something that
would dispel her anxiety
and put her mind at rest?

THE BURGLAR

There was a man here in the village
who chased girls to steal from them.
He didn't want money or anything
material. It was their personalities
he was after. He wanted their minds
and how their minds worked. Some
social gesture or mannerism that
he could make his own. Body language,
a tone of voice. The way they laughed.
How they used their eyes. The walls
of his mind came to be a gallery
of his thefts. He didn't harm the
girls but in his way he possessed
them. Few of them were aware of
what was happening when he moved
on to another prey. They attached
other reasons to his abandoning
them. How did it end? I don't
know, he moved away to another
town. His collection must be
vast by now, a huge mosaic.

SON IO L'AMORE

That's what she whispered to me
as we were walking beside the sea
near the abandoned Greek temple
of Paestum. I am love she told me
in an accent I could hardly understand.
A peasant girl who was tending a few sheep
in the meadow below the temple.
Not a beautiful girl but there was
such a radiance in her face.
Son io l'amore. She left her sheep
to graze and we walked along
the beach together in the summer warmth.
I didn't try to make love to her,
that would have been a desecration.
For a few moments she became a handmaiden
of the temple. Son io l'amore.
I never saw her again; I had to drive
to Salerno to meet friends.
That was half a century ago.
But now and then she enters my memory
and I hear her speaking in the accent
I can hardly understand. Son io l'amore.

VOICES IN THE NIGHT

Lately as I've been drifting
off into sleep I've been
hearing voices in the darkness
of my bedroom, voices that
I can't identify. One voice
is that of a woman (her
laugh is that of a woman)
and the other is a man's,
deeper in tone. Some nights
only one speaks. But often
they both talked, carrying
on a conversation. At first
I couldn't understand them,
but soon I got the hang of
their lingo. It was English
but a very formal English.
Their syntax wasn't modern;
it was old-fashioned, perhaps
the way people talked at the
turn of the century.

In their conversations they
often talked about another
person, a man who seemed to
have led an adventurous life
and who had been attracted
to women. The female
voice was very critical of
the way he had exploited
women. Apparently he had
been married three times
and had a series of love
affairs. The male voice

condoned his promiscuity,
even praised it. "A real
man," he said. One night
they got into an argument
about this fellow. "If
you'd only known him, how
awful he was, what an
egotist, how selfish." I
thought I caught a little
catch in her voice when
she said that. The male
voice just laughed.

Ordinarily I fell asleep
while the voices were
talking. But the other
night some things they
were saying startled me
awake. Talking about *him*
they said that he had lived
in Connecticut and that he
had published a book of
erotic verse. "Highbrow stuff,"
the male voice said, "full of
steamy classical allusions."

Could they be talking about me?
I was made certain of that
when the female voice recited
part of a poem, and it was one
of my poems:
    "He tried to make her
    understand that her
    body was part of his,
    which was what gave
    her her beauty and charm."

I stopped listening for their
voices. Now I turn up my bedside
radio to blot them out. I know
enough about myself already
without their help.

THE BREAD-KNIFE

Hugh MacDiarmid the voice
of the Scots revival wrote

in "The Kind of Poetry I
Want" that he dreamed "of

poems like the bread-knife
which cuts three slices at

once"   this puzzled me un-
til I read his biography

and realized that the knife
must be his hero Vladimir

Ilyich Lenin slicing thru
the sinews of capitalism

and he added "ah Lenin poli-
tics is child's play to what
this kind of poetry must be."

IN THE DARK WOOD

I'm dreaming, and as dusk falls
I see the figure of a tall man
coming toward me in the dark woods.
I recognize the figure as my father.
He looks to be in his late thirties,
about the time I was born. Yes,
my father, but he isn't wearing
his usual clothes, either his
dark suit for church or his
golfing outfit, a windbreaker
and knickers.

What he is wearing is very strange.
It's white and like a Roman toga,
reaching down to his ankles.
But he is barefoot. He's walking
very slowly, putting one foot
forward, a pause, and then
the other. When he comes around
a big oak I see why he's going
so slowly. Behind him, lying on
her belly, a woman is clutching
his legs. Each time he takes
a step she pulls herself
along the ground to follow him.
She is not wearing Roman dress
but a fashionable modern
evening gown. She has on
silk stockings and high-heeled
red slippers. She is wearing
a string of pearls. She looks
about twenty-five, as she would
have been when I was born.

A beautiful woman, as she is
in the full-length portrait
of my mother by Penrhyn
Stanlaws that hung at one
end of the dining room in
the house on Woodland Road.

I am so startled by this
apparition that I can't
speak to them. And if I could
what would I have to say to them?
Would I have asked him why
her frigidity mattered so
much to him that he took up
with other, and inferior,
women? Would I have asked
her why she didn't understand
that the others were merely
transient diversions?

I said nothing, and they
did not appear to see or
recognize me. It was an
agony for me to watch them,
slowly and painfully, abandon
me in that frighteningly
dark wood.

*"The Dark Wood": From Dante's "selva oscura" in the first strophe of
his Inferno.*

THE STRANGER

"They're only loaned to us,"
my grandmother told me, "and
before you know it there's
a person there." A person you
never knew before. In some
ways he's like you (perhaps
in the color of hair) but a
new person whom you have to
learn to love. But it's not
the kind of love which produced
the stranger. You have to
begin to learn about the
love the stranger needs and
wants. And you must learn
that often the stranger
will hurt you in ways you
at first can't understand.
You must accept the stranger
as he is because you made
him come to be.

ILLNESS

is a kind of prison in which the doctor
is the warden and the nurses are the guards.
There are no bars on the windows. It's not a
gloomy place; flowers make it bright and
cheerful. No court jury sets the length of
the sentences. That decision rests with
the warden, who prides himself on his
humanity. There are rules in his mind
which often seem arbitrary or confusing
to the prisoners. They can never tell
how long their incarceration will last.
It can be only a few days or it can be
a month or two. And there are some
prisoners who are never released at all;
dangerous cases. It is whispered on the
wards that they end up in the morgue.
I'm hoping that my stay will be short.
Though my cell is the most comfortable
I've ever had it's hard to bear or understand
Why I'm in it.

IN THE GOD'S DREAMS

Am I a character in the dreams
of the god Hermes the messenger?
Certainly many of my dreams
have nothing to do with the
common life around me. There
are never any automobiles or
airplanes in them. These
dreams belong to an age in
the distant past, to a time
perhaps when nothing was
written down, to the
time of memory.

I chose Hermes not out of
vanity but because from what
I've read about him he had a
pretty good time, was not
just a drunkard on Olympus.
In his traipsings delivering
divine messages he must have
met some pretty girls who
gave him pleasure. We know
that he invented the lyre
for the benefit of poets,
and Lucian relates in his
Dialogues of the Dead that
he was the god of sleep
and dreams.

My dreams are not frightening,
they are not nightmares. But
their irrationality puzzles
me. What is Hermes trying to

tell me? Is he playing a game
with me? Last Monday night
I dreamt about a school for
young children who had heads
but no bodies. Last night it
was a cow that was galloping
in our meadow like a horse.
Another night, and this one
was a bit scary, I swam across
the lake with my head under
water, I didn't have to breathe air.

What is the message of these
dreams? Into what kind of world
is Hermes leading me? It's not
the world described daily in the
New York Times. A world of
shadows? A kind of levitation?

How can I pray to Hermes to lay
off these senseless fantasies,
tell him that I want *real* dreams
such as my shrink can explicate.

I've looked up lustration in
the dictionary. Its definition
is not encouraging: "a prefatory
ceremony, performed as a preliminary
to entering a holy place." That's
too impersonal. I want a man-to-man
talk with Hermes, telling him to
stop infesting my nights with
his nonsense.

HER LIFE

is the lives of the birds. She
watches them by the hour from her
kitchen window as they peck for
the food she has put out for them
in the feeder. The food they like
best comes in 25-lb. sacks, too
heavy for her to lift, she has to
have UPS bring it. She keeps the
grains in a garbage can, scooping them
out with a ladle as she needs it.

Many kinds of birds come to her
feeder. Sparrows, mourning doves,
chickadees, blue jays that frighten
the smaller birds; thrushes, blue-
birds that have their own house
perched on the fence rail; humming-
birds, juncos, rose-breasted
grosbeaks, finches, and some that
she can't identify in her bird
guide. She is sad when winter comes
and some of her friends take off
for the south.

The birds are her comfort; they
help her to go on with her life,
which has been hard to bear. Her
beloved husband died three years
before from cancer, a hard death.
And now her son has married a
vulgar woman who thinks only
of money. But she has her dear
birds. They comfort her. They
come every day and never let
her down.

THE WEIGHT GUESSER

One summer when he was college
age he had a job as a weight
guesser in a traveling carnival.
If he could guess a person's
weight within ten pounds he
would win ten dollars. But if
he was off by ten pounds
he had to fork over a ten-spot.
He got pretty good at the guessing
and made money over the summer.

But later in life when he
was interested in a girl
and wanted to make out with her
he found that the system didn't
work very well. The girl he
wanted was more concerned in his
valuation of her charm and beauty
than being weighed.

I CANNOT SEPARATE HER

from the beautiful body.
She has charm and a very
gay spirit; in every way
she's attractive. Intelligent
and she reads good books.
But it's the faultless body
that forces me to make a fool
of myself, pursuing a virtuous
girl I could never possess.

THE VISITOR

When I closed my eyes I could see
the head of a girl in half-light.
But was it you? She had your
aristocratic arch of the neck
and your pretty curls, but where
were your laugh and your sparkle?
And your glance toward me wasn't
particularly affectionate.

I ran through the catalog of
past loves but this girl was
not there. She must have been you.
But the frown? How had I
displeased you? Please tell me,
but then visions can't talk.

The telephone rang: I opened
my eyes to go answer it. Drat!
It was the broker who wants me
to buy Bell Atlantic stock.
I went back to the sofa to close
my eyes again. But you were
gone, perhaps never to reappear.

THE FIXATION

*"A woman's breasts bear the paradoxical
burden of being aesthetic organs."*

His English governess could undress
or dress without removing her outer
garment. The child asked her why she did that
but she wouldn't offer an explanation.
He learned something important when little
Yerma, the girl next-door, led him into
the bushes to show him her nipples.

He didn't learn much more until he
and his brother were on the night
train from Pittsburgh to New York.
In those days there were Pullman
sleeping cars in which the porters
made lower and upper berths,
separated by heavy green curtains.
He was in an upper berth, his
brother was across the aisle.

When he was settled in his berth
and had changed into his pajamas
he noted that light was coming
from the adjacent lower berth.
The porter hadn't closed the
curtains tightly. He looked
down through the gap and saw
a lady who was naked, no nightgown
or anything on. She was leaning
against her pillows playing with
her . . . he didn't know what to
call them then. They were soft
and beautiful and hung down as far

as her tummy. At the end of them
were little pink circles with
buttons that stood up when she
touched them.

When he heard the porter walking
down the aisle he pulled back his
head and stopped looking. He never
told his brother what he had seen,
but as he grew up the sight of the
lady never left his memory. It was
his secret that he carried into
adulthood and even into old age.

"A woman's breasts . . .": Natalie Angier, from a review in the
    New York Times *of Marilyn Yalon's book,* A History of the
    Breast.

HER MEMORY BANK

It has no entrance. For years
I walked past the building
But could never find how to get in.
As I go past the windows
I can see clerks piling up
Stacks of money, but there is
No way to get at it, the money
I need so badly.

I enquire about the memory bank,
But none of my friends has ever
Heard of it. They think I'm crazy
Or hallucinating. They tap
A finger to their heads when
I ask about the memory bank.

They say there is no such bank,
But I know better. I have some
Wonderful memories from your
Memory bank and I want more.

LOVE SONG

As we lived together
it dawned on me from

little things she said
or did there had been

lovers before me, but
it didn't matter. For

me she was always fresh
as a daisy and has so

remained in my heart
all the years we have

been parted, fresh as a
daisy through the years.

THE MAN WHO
FOLLOWED ME

Often last year I was down in the
village, walking let's say from
the pharmacy to the post office
or the grocery, when I noticed
that a young man, a stranger,
seemed to be following me. I'd
never seen him before in the
village, where everyone usually
knows everyone else. Our village
is a small one. When I approached
this fellow, who was wearing a
leather jacket over a T-shirt,
he didn't stop to talk to me
but took off through the bushes
on the slope below the town hall.
I asked about him there and at
the post office, but nobody had
seen him or knew anything about him.

This fellow didn't show up every
day but he would appear two or
three times a week, though never
on Sundays. He got on my nerves.
Finally I'd had enough and ran
back to accost him. I asked who
he was and what he wanted with me.
He raised a hand, almost a menacing
gesture, and replied in a voice
that was like a groan. "Don't you
recognize me? You've known me
most of your life." And then he
was off into the bushes. It was

eerie and it was frightening.
What kind of a supernatural
trap was I getting into?

The apparitions continued intermittently.
I was almost beginning to accept them,
without fear. Then there was a news
story in the *Winsted Citizen* about
the body of a young man, who could
not be identified, which had been
found drowned in Mad River which
runs with great force through Winsted.

I couldn't resist visiting the coroner's
office. One glance at the corpse under
the rubber sheet and I knew it was
my pursuer, though his face was contorted
in agony. They said he would be buried
in a pauper's grave. I certainly didn't
want him. But I still wonder whether
he was a part of me, a part that
I didn't want to remember.

THE REPRISE

I'm very old now
and my strength is failing
but I want to make love with you
before I die. It couldn't be
the wild love-making of youth
I'm beyond that now.
But let it be quiet love,
touching and kissing,
the pressing together
of our naked bodies.
I want to kiss you all over
in every part of your
beautiful body, every
lovely inch of it.
And please touch me
the way you used to do.
I want to make love with you
before I die.

DESDEMONA'S
HANDKERCHIEF

caused a mass of mischief
that ended in her death.
Beware my beloved lady
let not jealousy poison
our happiness. I am as weak,
as prone to fantasy
as any lover. Don't put me
to the test. Lock up your
handkerchiefs where no
malicious meddler
can find them.

DIANA'S SELF MIGHT TO THESE WOODS RESORT

It all happened (if it happened at all)
many centuries ago, but when I saw you
in your untouched purity, I knew that
the old myth was true, that you, Diana,
were wandering innocently in the woods
until the amorous god pursued you and
irrevocably altered your being.

Title: a line from Purcell's opera Dido and Aeneas.

LOVE DOES NOT MAKE A DISPLAY
OF ITSELF

But when you finally think you've met Miss Right
it's hard to keep the lid on.
You try not to let your friends know
what has happened, in case something goes wrong.
Was it a mistake to take her to Paris for a week
before we got married? Something strange
happened in the restaurant on the Eiffel Tower.
We were sitting at a table with a view;
we were looking down at the meandering Seine
and the Champs de Mars with Napoleon's tomb.
She seemed to be enjoying herself
but suddenly she stopped smiling and talking
and her eyes went glazed. It was as if
I was a stranger who had offended her.
I had the feeling that she didn't know who I was.
When this mood went on for two days
I flew her back to New York, where her mother
took over. Her mother made her go to a shrink
but the pills and therapy didn't do any good.
I brought flowers for her every day,
anemones, her favorite flower,
but she never spoke to me or seemed
to recognize me. Her father got me alone
to tell me that we weren't suited for each other.
I guess the shrink told him that.
He said he was breaking off our engagement
and that I was not to try to see her again.
Love does not make a display of itself.
Was that what, in my happiness, I had done
without knowing it? I was so crazy about her
I guess I didn't realize the effect on her.

Title: a line from the Episcopal marriage service.

LOST BRAINS

He felt as if his brains
were jumping out of his head.
It had begun when he saw her
flirting with another man
at a party. The man was a
nobody who liked to pick up
girls. She swore that no one
else meant anything to her.
But when it happened again,
this time in a crowded bar,
his head started spinning
and he knew that his brain
was going to jump out through
his ears. Without her he would
become a nobody too.

"He felt . . . his head": The line is from the British film Dance
    with a Stranger.

NUNC DIMITTIS

Little time now
and so much hasn't
been put down as I
should have done it.
But does it matter?
It's all been written
so well by my betters,
and what they wrote
has been my joy.

"HARRY"

The Death of Harry Levin

This whole sad business of a friend's dying.
What box does that go in among the storage spaces
    in my head?
Filed not alphabetically, not chronologically,
    scattered boxes piled where they dropped
      when there was a death, no markings on them.

Harry. My grief, and perhaps his relief that
    there's no more pain to be gotten through.
    His face on the obituary page of the *Times*
    is serene and confident.
What later happens to him, the superb stylist
    and paragon of scholars, will be to his
    credit.
So I still see him in the small neat house
    where over the years
I've most often come to talk with him,
The best advisor an unschooled young
    publisher could have.
He will be sitting composed and erect
    at his workdesk.
Unlike my desk at home, his desk has
    no books or papers piled up on it.
He gives the sense that anything he
    might want to refer to is in his head.
The students whisper about his
    photographic memory.
They boast of it to students in other
    courses as if it were their own.
I myself never took a course with him;
Nevertheless, when he had the time
He was ready to advise me about
Books I should publish at New Directions.

FATA MORGANA

Like the weather, her visits were
uncertain. Often I would wait for
weeks, fearing I had lost her.
Then, toward midnight, there would
be a scratching at my door. She
never knocked, she would scratch
like a cat with her long nails, and
I awakened myself for pleasure,
for the generosity with which
she dispensed her charms.

She spoke a little English but
she would never tell me about
herself, whence she came or
what her history had been.
To this day I know only the
mysterious radiance of her
being, how when I held her
in my arms she could unleash
an unbridled passion.

She would never stay with me
for long. Then, with a kiss
she would be off. Where was
she going when she left me?
Was there another lover, or
lovers, waiting for her visit?
Nor did she ever tell me her
name. So, to myself, I call
her Fata Morgana, the best
loved of King Arthur's
damsels.

FUNERALS

in our village are short and to the point.
While the mourners are finding their seats
Etta Andrews plays "Now the Day Is Over."
No one is ashamed to wipe his or her eyes.
Then the Reverend stands up and reads
the Lord's Prayer with the mourners
speaking it with him. Then there is a hymn,
usually "Rock of Ages" or one chosen by
the wife of the deceased. The deceased,
I might say, is never present, except for
an urn prepared by Mr. Torrant, who is
always squinting. Next there are remarks
by the Reverend. He is a kind man and
can be relied upon to say something nice
about the life of the departed, no matter
how much he may have been scorned or even
disliked.

The Reverend's eulogies are so much the
same, with appropriate readings from scripture,
that I gave up listening to them years ago.
Instead, unheard, I eulogize myself,
the real picture of how I've been in
the village. I admit that I was self-satisfied
and arrogant. I didn't go to much pains
to provide diversions for my wife. When
the children and grandchildren came for visits
I lectured them and pointed out their faults.
I made appropriate contributions to the
local charities but without much enthusiasm.
I snubbed people who bored me and avoided
parties. I was considerate to the people
who worked in the post office. I complained

a great deal about my ailments. When I'm
asked how I'm doing, I reply that I'm
not getting any younger. This inveterate
response has become a bore in the village.

After the Reverend's eulogy is over
there is another hymn, and the benediction.
As they leave everyone, except me, presses
the flesh of the bereaved with appropriate
utterances. But I get away as quickly as
I can. If they don't bore me I like
almost all the people in the village.
But as they go, I tick them off. I've
been to at least fifty funerals. When
will mine be?

BOOK II

THE LAST POEM TO BE WRITTEN

"When, when & whenever
death closes our eyes"

still shall I behold her
smiling such brightness

lady of brightness &
the illumined heart

soft walker in my blood
snow color sea sound

track of the ermine
delicate in the snow

line of the sea wave
delicate on the sand

lady of all brightness
donna del mio cuor.

"*Quandocumquigitur nostros mors claudet ocellos*":
Propertius in the "Nox mihi candida."

IN ANOTHER COUNTRY

tesoro

she would say with that succulent
accent on the middle o as if she
were holding something as precious
as the golden testicle of a god.

Credere!

OBBEDIRE! COMBATTERE! I guess
it was the same then every-
where all over Italy in big
white letters painted up on

walls and especially on railroad
retaining walls at the
grade crossings and to make
a good record and show how

things were in ordine they
would let down the crossing
bars ten minutes before the
trains came so people were

backed up on both sides in
crowds shouting across to
each other all a big joke
and that's how we met where

we first saw each other I
was on the up side walking
back to town from swimming
& she was on the other with

her bicycle heading to the
cove wearing her tight white
sweater with nothing under
it & her grey checked skirt

& sandals era come Beatrice
al ponte quando si videro la
prima volta there by that
bridge in Florence where he

first saw her (later one day
she brought her schoolbook
of Dante so I could see the
famous painting) com' allora

al ponte only neither of us
was shy first we were look-
ing then we were smiling and
when the train had finally

passed and we met in the mid-
dle I just took hold of her bi-
cycle and walked beside her
but you have swum already I

can see your hair's all wet
why do you want to go again?
why do you think? I said ma
brutta I'm ugly sono brutta

and at the cove she changed
behind a big rock into her
suit it was white and tight
too ti piace? she asked you

like it? the water was very
clear that day and the rocks
were warm there was a German
boy came nosing around but

she wasn't nice to him and
he went away after we swam
we sat on the rocks sunning
& talking I only knew a few

words of Italian then but we
found another language that
did well enough I'd draw a
picture of the word I wanted

with my finger on her thigh
or she on mine the sky was
clear the air was soft with
just a little breeze I was

18 she was 15 and her name
was Leontina going back to
town she had me ride her on
the handlebars and put her

arms around my neck to keep
from falling off she didn't
want an icecream mamma m'as–
petta alla casa my mother's

waiting for me so I'd better
go just leave me here ma se
tu vuoi 'sta sera dopo la
passeggiata al angolo near

the newsstand quando sono
le nove yes I said yes I'll
be there alle nove after the
churchbells sound at nine.

Giacomino!

she called vieni qua splashing her
arms in the clear green water vieni
subito and so I followed her swim-
ming around a point of rock to the

next cove vieni qua non hai paura
and she slipped like an eel beneath
the surface down through the sunken
entrance to a hidden grotto where

the light was soft and green on fine-
grained sand è bello no? here we can
be together by ourselves nobody else
has ever been here with me it's my se-

cret place here kiss me here I found
it when I was a little girl now touch
me here è strano questa luce com' un
altro mondo so strange this light am

I all green? it's like another world
does that feel good? don't be afraid
siamo incantati we're enchanted in
another world O Giacomino Giacomino

sai tu amore come lui è bello? com' è
carino sai quanto tu mi dai piacere?
sai come lei ti vuol' bene? lie still
non andare via just lie still lie still.

Genovese

non sono I'm Roman it comes from
my father look at my nose it went
straight down from her forehead
like coins you see from Etruria.

Tornerai?

she wept will you come back
for me I wanted to slip away
but she found out the time
of the train and was there

in the compartment wearing
her Sunday dress & the Mil-
anese scarf I had given her
tornerai amore mio will you

come back and bring me to
America crying and pressing
my hands against her breasts
my face wet with her tears

& her kisses till the train
stopped at Genova and they
made her get off because I
couldn't buy her a ticket.

THE BIRD OF ENDLESS TIME

Your fingers touch me like a bird's wing
like the feathers of the bird that returns

every hundred years to brush against a
peak in the Himalayas and not until the

rock's been worn away will time and the
kalpas end   why do I think of the fable

when I'm close with you   surely because
I want so many lives to feel your touch.

KALPA: *in Hinduism, an eon, a vast period of time that encompasses the
creation and dissolution of a universe.*

THE SEARCH

She writes that she cannot
Find me in her dreams. She
Has been searching for me
Night after night but with
No success. "Why are you
Hiding from me?" she asks,
"Did I do something to
Offend you, to hurt you?
I think you must have
Misunderstood what was
Meant as a sign of love."

"Look further, look deeper,"
I write her. "The world of
Dreams is vast. It has many
Passageways that lead to
Corners no one has ever
Visited. Don't abandon the
Search too easily. Don't
Give up. I have encountered
You in *my* dreams, beautiful
As you always were, your
Voice the same, unchanged.

"Yet what difference does
It make where we meet, in
Your dreams or in mine?
Does it matter if we are
Insubstantial? We still
Can speak the words we
Know, the words of love."

EYES ARE THE GUIDES
OF LOVE

said Propertius oculi sunt
in amore duces so why does

she close them yet her lips
are open (in a smile) as if

they were her eyes dulce ri-
dentem so I shall not re-

proach the secrecy of her
eyes though she does not

tell me what it is perhaps
it isn't for me to know.

HAVING FAILED

with every other stratagem
should I now try jealousy

taunting you in these ver-
ses that you have been sup-

planted it would be useless
every messenger from Boeotia

to Samos would report that
my bed is still empty that

the lamp burns for me alone.

TO BE SURE

there are other fish in
the sea but why are the

loveliest fish so often
virtuous o poluphlois-

boios thalasses release
I beseech you strong po-

tions of passionate love
into your winedark waves.

I HATE LOVE

says Alcaeus echthairo ton
erota and Rufinus boasts

that he has armed himself
against love with wisdom

hoplismai pros erota peri
sternaoisi logismon and

Meleager weeps his woes
to the night and his bed–

lamp hiere kai luchne and
these are wise words from

men of experience but alas
I am caught in that trap

for Eraclea has put her
little foot on my neck

and I cannot heed them.

LIKE THE OCTOPUS

I would enfold you in my
tentacles but believe me

my embrace is loving not
injurious some say that

to confuse his prey the
octopus sends out a kind

of ink to cloud the wa-
ter so too the poet e-

mits ink (much ink) on
his beloved but it is

not noxious his poems
may be bad but their in-

tention is affectionate
they are part of his oc-

topode nature they are his
submarine squeak of love.

BEFORE I DIE

(for Jeanine Lambert)

I want to ride once more on
the Paris Métro Madeleine

Vendôme Palais Royal I
used to know by heart the

names of the Métro sta-
tions between where I lived

and where you lived and I
still smell the sweet odor

of the cars (they used to
spray them every night to

freshen them up) it was a
smell of death   you died

of cancer at twenty   I did-
n't learn of it till much

later   I was working out in
India   Saint Germain Sainte

Chapelle Palais de Justice
I called on your family

and heard the sad story
while your mother and fa-

ther wept   Châtelet Hôtel
de Ville Bastille   Jean-

ine Jeanine adorable Jean-
ine I want to ride again

in the Métro   I think I'll
find you there waiting

to laugh and sit beside
me and hold my hand.

THE ENLACEMENT

There's something holy about
falling asleep pressed close

against a beloved   is it a sur-
vival from some primitive rite

it's more than the huddling
together of animals in the

storm   is one body a sanctu-
ary for another   the enlace-

ment's a vow for the future
a pledge not to be broken

now blood touches blood and
breath breath as if they were

hands touching and holding.

MANY LOVES

She changes the way
she does her hair for
each new admirer. If
she is to have many
loves she wants to be
a different person
for each one of them.

AN ANGINAL EQUIVALENT

For those little stabs of pain
in the region of the heart the

poet is having an EKG   the wires
are attached to a small TV and

as he lies there he can watch
the bouncing beat on the screen

qualim asks Martial velim quae-
ris nolimve puellam? nolo nimis

facilem difficilemque nimis what
does that jerking line tell him

about the prospect for his new
affection illud quod medium est

atque inter utrumque probamus
nec volo quod cruciat nec volo

quod satiat which will she be?

You ask what kinds of girl I like and don't like
Let her not be a pushover, yet not too hard to get
Somewhere between the two
Not one who tears me to pieces
But not one who hangs on my neck.
                                    —MARTIAL I, lvii

SONG

O lovely lovely so lovely
just fresh from a night of

it lovely oh I saw you at
nine in the morning coming

home in the street with no
hat and your coat clutched

tight but not hiding your
evening dress lovely and

fresh from a night of it
lovely you stopped on the

curb for the light & your
eye caught mine lovely so

lovely and you knew that
I knew and you knew that

I wanted you too so fresh
from a night of it lovely.

THE HAPPY POETS

It's my delight to recite
my poems in the arms of

an intelligent girl and
to please her sweet ear

with what I have written.

Me iuvet in gremio doctae legisse puellae
auribus et puris scripta probasse mea
               —PROPERTIUS II, xiii

And Goethe boasts that he
tapped out his hexameters

on the back of his Roman
girlfriend while she slept.

Und des Hexameters Mass leise mit fingern der Hand
Ihr auf den Rücken gezählt. Sie atmet in lieblichem Schlummer.
Und es durchglühet ihr Hauch mir bis ins Tiefste die Brust.
               —GOETHE, Römische Elegien V

IN THE MUSEUM AT TEHERAN

a sentimental curator has placed
two fragments of bronze Grecian
   heads together boy

and girl so that the faces black-
ened by the three thousand years of
   desert sand & sun

seem to be whispering something
that the Gurgan lion & the wing-
   ed dog of Azerbaijan

must not hear but I have heard
them as I hear you now half way
   around the world

so simply & so quietly more like
a child than like a woman making
   love say to me in

that soft lost near and distant voice
I'm happy now I'm happy oh don't
   move don't go away.

THE SUMMONS

He went out to their glorious war
and went down in it and his
    last belief was

her love as he breathed flame
in the waves and sank burning
    now I lie under

his picture in the dark room
in the wife's bed and partake
    of his unknown

life does he see does he stand
in the room does he feel does
    he burn again?

later I wake in the night while
she sleeps and call out to him
    wanderer come

return to this bed and embody the
love that was yours and is hers
    and is mine
    and endures.

A LONG NIGHT OF DREAMING

and when I finally awoke
from it we seemed to be

back where we'd left off
some thirty years before

in the compartment of a
wagon-lit somewhere in

Italy loving and arguing
soft words and then hard

words over where we'd go
next to Venice to Rome or

better to split again you
back to him I back to her.

LONG AND LANGUOROUS

A whole stolen afternoon before us
no hurry no haste   savoring every

sensation   begin perhaps with mimi-
cry of memories of adolescence

what you learned from the boy next
door what the lady who was divorced

taught me   no hurry no haste   how
is it that lovemaking from long ago

can return so vividly   we can still
feel certain touches hear certain

tones of voice even remember some
of the words exchanged   making love

is cumulative   nothing of it that
was good is really lost   and yet

there can always be discoveries
little hidden paths to pleasure

no haste no hurry   time for a mo-
ment's doze between enlacements

time even for a bit of joking be-
cause there is that aspect of the

ridiculous in coupling   better it
all be soft and slow gentle and

generous as our afternoon speeds
on its way long and languorous.

WE MET IN A DREAM

some forty years ago there on your
ermo colle in the hills behind Rec-

anati with its hedgerow cutting off
the view of the horizon you instruct-

ed me in morality and we talked of the
great dead of Plotinus and Copernicus

and of many another then came a third
who sought to join us and we welcomed

him readily for he spoke of love and
of desire and of a man who became a

city much we conversed together in
dreams through many nights but in

the end we thought only of the no-
thingness of the infinite nothing-

ness parlando del naufragar in questo
mare of sweet drowning under the great

falls of the river of drowning in the
love that is beyond all earthly love.

ANIMA MEA

After we had made love
a girl with big eyes and
warm breath started to
talk about my soul hush
I said hush and beware
if I have a soul it's
only a box of vanities
tied with frightened
pieces of string.

ANIMA MEA: *my soul.*

THE CAVE

Leaning over me her hair
makes a cave around her

face a darkness where her
eyes are hardly seen she

tells me she is a cat she
says she hates me because

I make her show her pleas-
ure she makes a cat-hate

sound and then ever so
tenderly hands under my

head raises my mouth into
the dark cave of her love.

NEAR ZERMATT: THE DRAHTSEILBAHN

(for Maria)

High over the deep
alpine valley a load
is climbing the thin

wire to the village
that clings to the
mountainside under

the cliffs & my love
rides up to you on
such a thin thread

of hope trembling in
empty space over the
chasm that seems so

bottomless drawn up–
ward drawn upward
because you are there

so distant so close
and will always be
there far above me.

INTO EACH LIFE

must fall occasionally a new
incentive to persist he writes

ridiculous letters to ces dames
galantes well what's the harm

in that he searches for the
ear that comprehends the in-

tonations that he hears in
languages he tells her that

her hands when she is talking
are the white flock of birds

En Bertrans saw that day be-
yond the battlements of Haute-

fort (touch is not necessary
for the delectations of the

mind the poet saw her only
once the old book says there

at the bridge over the Arno).

AT THE BOULE D'OR

As they lunch together at
the Boule d'Or they are

smiling a lot and choosing
their words carefully   this

is their first date & each
is trying to impress   they

are feeling each other out
and weighing the potentials

(her beauty & his capacity
for making money)   now they

are laughing & talking with
more animation   they find

they like each other   but
can either foresee the bit-

ter words that will follow?

THE SECRETS

The secrets of your body
are difficult to unlock
and difficult to solve.
I see you moving about
the house or walking in
the garden; your movements
are ordinary. But when I
watch you closely sometimes
I sense that certain gestures
of your body, quite apart
from what you may be saying,
are eluding my understanding.
These are rare qualities
of your physical being.

How may I define what I
observe? My feelings as I
watch you are so tenuous,
so vague. Should I even be
concerned about these strange
perceptions? Is my mind
afloat in wanderings? How
could your body's secrets
harm me? It's not as if you
had a contagious disease?

Perhaps it's I who have a
disease: a longing for
complete knowledge and
possession. Probably that's
what makes me so curious
about the secrets of
your body.

ALBA

I tell the birds you can stop now
I no longer need you I wake to a

more lovely music she has been
speaking to me in my dreams the

birds protest that it has always
been their task to arouse me for

the day do not disturb our lives
they say very well I tell them

you may still sing at dawn but
only in her praise you must imi-

tate her voice or I'll not listen
I will be deaf to your song.

IN HALF DARKNESS

your face is still so beautiful
there is a different radiance

that comes in sleep   I wake and
touch your cheek   I feel your

breath on my groping fingers
your eyes are closed but I sus-

pect they can see & are watch-
ing what is to come   they are

looking into the future as far
as the end of our time together.

THE DARKENED ROOM

Night is a room darkened for lovers.
The sun is gone, and our daytime concerns
And distractions with it.
Now in the darkness we are close together
As lovers are meant to be.
Whether we sleep or wake
Nothing intrudes between us.
We are soothed and protected
By the darkness of our room.

"Night is a room darkened for lovers": from William Carlos Williams,
"Complaint."

THE INVISIBLE PERSON

Life kept rolling her over
like a piece of driftwood

in the surf of an angry sea
she was intelligent and beau-

tiful and well-off she made
friends easily yet she wasn't

able to put the pieces to-
gether into any recognizable

shape   she wasn't sure who
she wanted to be   so she

ended up being no one in par-
ticular   she made herself al-

most invisible   she was the
person you loved so much who

really wasn't there at all.

THE REVENANTS

At a table in the corner two people
are talking in low voices a young

man and a girl   they call each other
Paolo & Francesca   if they are reven-

ants they are at least 800 years old
perhaps more (who knows   there are

no birth certificates for revenants
or passports which limit where they

may go) they are speaking in an al-
most forgotten language   seriously

quietly sadly as if once they had had
great sorrow (were they perhaps sepa-

rated in the lower world) sad chil-
dren of another time   have they re-

turned here to find each other again
now and then the girl smiles for an

instant in a puzzled way   he takes
her hand they go on talking softly.

. . . Nessun maggior dolore
Che ricordarsi del tempo felice
Ne la miseria . . .
—DANTE, Inferno, V, 121–23

THE AFTERTHOUGHT

When he had driven her
to JFK so she could fly

back to Zurich for her
next film and they had

brother–sisterly kissed
goodbye (he feared they

might never meet again
he worked only in Hol-

lywood) she ran back
through the gate to

say in her crazy Swiss
German du weisch weisch

du nöt dass diene chatz-
li-and-müessli Schpiël

mir a ganz grosse Freud
gmacht hänt es war chaiba

güet   you know that I did
love the bed part too it

was great   then she had
rushed off to her flight

one of his life's precious
moments that he would

treasure long as he lived.

A SECRET LANGUAGE

I wish I could talk to your body
less cautiously I mean in a

language as forthright as its
beauty deserves of course

when we make love there is the
communication of touch fingers

on flesh lips on innermost
flesh but surely there must be

a kind of speech body in body
that is even deeper than such

surface touching a language
I haven't yet learned or haven't

learned well enough hard as
I've tried will I ever master

that secret language for you?

WHAT IS IT MAKES
ONE GIRL

more lovely than all others
it is the light within omne

quod manifestatur lumen est
a fructive light that shines

within the radiance of the il-
lumined heart risplende in sè

perpetuale effecto the light
descending to her from sun

moon and stars lux enim per se
in omnem partem se ipsam dif-

fundit the light of the ima-
gination the light that wakes

and shines the light of love.

NOTHING THAT'S LOVELY
CAN MY LOVE ESCAPE

How many cowgirls did the
blue God Krishna love doz-

ens the old books say and
so it is with me nothing

that's lovely can my love
escape like Baby Krishna

for his butter ball I'm
greedy greedy greedy I

was not born like Krishna
on a lotus leaf but yet I

want to play as he did in
his palm grove long ago.

SHE'S NOT EXACTLY LIKE YOU

so she won't do   and when the Lady Maeut
had rejected Bertrand de Born sens totas

ochaisos without any reason and he knew
he would never find another like her que

valha vos qu'ai perduda he said he would
never love again ja mais no vuolh aver

druda and in his poem Domna puois de me
no-us chal he borrowed graces from seven

other ladies from Cembelis and Aelis from
the chatelaine of Chalais and the fair-

tressed Agnes from the one he called Better-
than-Good (Mielhs-de-be) from Audiart

and the toothsome Faidida from the mirror
lady (who was she?) but taken all together

they could not equal Maeut and so it is
with me there is no other to replace you

no sai on m'enquieira there's nowhere I
would look que ja mais non er per me tan

rics jais for never will there be so
rich a joy or a lady who pleases me so.

EROS AS ARCHAEOLOGIST

searches the ruins of my youth
he finds shards from half-for-

gotten loves old baubles that
once gleamed   a comb from soft

hair a broken mirror a worn
glove lost one winter's day

a sandal left on the beach
it is a melancholy midden

that he screens & must I
see myself in this debris

now that the only one
I want to see is you?

A TRANSLATION

How did you decide to translate me
from one language to another   let's

say from the English of friendship
to the French of lovers   we'd known

each other half a year when one day
as we were talking (it was about one

of your drawings) suddenly you curl-
ed yourself against me and drew my

lips down to yours   it was so deft
an alternance from one language to

the other as if to say yes you can
speak French to me now if you wish.

THE SINKING STONE

(for Maria)

High in the alpine
snowfields when a

stone slips from a
peak and rolls to

the glacier below
the sun will heat

it in the burning
days of spring and

it will melt itself
a hole & disappear

in the snow I like
that stone burned

hot from loving you
am sinking deep in-

to a cold vast no-
where ice land of

your loving someone
else instead of me!

IN HAC SPE VIVO

My head can lend no succour
to my heart because her face

is beyond all wonder she is
like diamond to glass when

her eyelids part their frin-
ges of bright gold and when

to the lute she sings she
makes the nightbird mute

gods why do you make us love
your goodly gifts and snatch

them right away I marvel how
the fish do live in the sea

but patience gazes on the
graves of kings (and mine).

OUR MEETINGS

Where do our thoughts meet
after we have sent them to

each other down the sidere-
al pathways   will they come

together again at Vrindavan
where Radha and the blue god

Krishna loved & are loving

    Let the earth of my body be mixed
    with the earth my beloved walks on
    Let the fire of my body be the brightness
    in the mirror that reflects his face
    Let the water of my body join the waters
    of the lotus pool he bathes in

will they meet again on the
black ship where Tristan and

la belle Iseut sang mournfully

    Sehnender Minne
    schwellendes Blühen
    schmachtender Liebe
    seliges Glühen
    Jach in der Brust
    jauchzende Lust

or in the castle of Montagnac
above the Vezère where En Ber-
tran pursued the fair Maheut

Domna puois de me no-us chal
e partit m'avetz de vos
sens totas ochaisos
no sai on m'enquieira
que ja mais
non er per me tan rics jais
cobratz   e si del semblan
no trop domna a mon talan
que valha vos qu'ai perduda
ja mais no vuolh aver druda

Our thoughts have met at many
times in many places   through

divers bodies have we joined
our thoughts   so often before

now have we lived this love.

The translation from the Bengali of Radha's hymn to Krishna is from
Levertov & Dimock, In Praise of Krishna.
The duet in German is from Act 1, *Scene* 5 *of Wagner's libretto for*
Tristan and Isolde.

> *Passionate longing-song*
> *Swelling and blooming*
> *Languishing love*
> *glow of high bliss*
> *deep in the heart*
> *jubilant desire . . .*

Bertrand de Born's compleynte when Maheut de Montagnac has given
him the gate follows the text of Roubaud's anthology, Les Trou-
badours.

Lady, since you no longer care for me
and have sent me away for no reason
I don't know where to look for love
because never will there be such rich joy for me
or ever found again in your likeness
Since there cannot be a lady the equal
of the one I've lost
I never want to have a lover again.

87

BOOK III

O BEST OF ALL NIGHTS,
RETURN AND RETURN AGAIN

How she let her long hair down over her shoulders, making a love
    cave around her face. Return and return again.

How when the lamplight was lowered she pressed against him, twin-
    ing her fingers in his. Return and return again.

How their legs swam together like dolphins and their toes played like
    little tunnies. Return and return again.

How she sat beside him cross-legged, telling him stories of her child-
    hood. Return and return again.

How she closed her eyes when his were open, how they breathed to-
    gether, breathing each other. Return and return again.

How they fell into slumber, their bodies curled together like two
    spoons. Return and return again.

How they went together to Otherwhere, the fairest land they had
    ever seen. Return and return again.

O best of all nights, return and return again.

After the Pervigilium Veneris *and Propertius's "Nox mihi candida."*

THE DECONSTRUCTED MAN

Multas per gentes et multa per aequora vectus
(et multas per vias quoque aereas)
(there being no flugbuggies in the time of Gaius Velerius)
through many lands by shores of many peoples
a life too short sometimes
at times a life too long-seeming
the days of sun and rain and many days of mountain snow
the nights of endless dreaming
my periplum more geographically extended
(in Java the airplane is the god Garuda)
but I learned less not being polumetis
and my paideuma is a mishmash of contradictions
my Circes a list of fictions

Muse help me to sing
of Toodles on the wide beach at Troorak
(her hair so golden and her brain so slack)
of darling Leontina di Rapallo
taking me to her underwater cave
(J'ai rêvé dans la grotte où nage la sirène
I have lingered in the chambers of the sea)
of Dylan's crazy Daphne in the Gargoyle Club in Soho
(Voi che sapete che cosa è amor . . .
Sento un affeto pien di desir
ch'ora è diletto ch'ora è martir)
of delicate moonlit Delia by the Strait of Juan DeFuca
of Cynthia whom I helped the gods destroy
in ogne parte dove mi trae memoria
of name-is-gone-but-not-her-smile
there in the jungle near Chichén Itzá
(A ristorar le pene d'un innocente amor)
of Kyo-San (they had girl caddies on the course at Kamakura)
(Ma in Ispagna son già mille e tre)

a list of fictions of beautiful contradictions
Lord Krishna's lotus and Williams' asphodel
each one so wonderful so new bringing her particular magic
risplende ognun sa luce che non morirà mai
and Restif said there were a thousand women who were always one
sola et magna (mater)
Gertrude's Mother of us All
I penetrate thy temple and thou doest my soul restore
ineffable thou art the Virgin & the Whore
I lusted for Tom's Wendy in Kentucky there was guilt
his sin (if it were sin for him) but surely mine
a list of fictions of contradictions
ma basta per oggi il catalogo delle fanciulle
who cares though I cared everywhere and always
the sea was not my mother but my mother took me to the sea
the old Cunarder Mauretania and Bill the sailor
who showed me how to splice a rope
and Jack turned green when we were beating through the chop
    above Grenada
avoid the Indian Ocean you can die of heat
posh P & O boats are like baking ovens
the sea the sea cried Xenophon after his weary march
O mother sea our bodies turn to dust our hearts return to thee
but it's the air we breathe and now in the air we fly
what would the many-crafted Odysseus make of that
he never saw as I have seen from the cabin window of the plane
glistening Mont Blanc and holy Kanchenjunga and mystic Fuji
by Isfahan he never saw those traceries
of ancient water tunnels on the desert below
he did not see the million lights of cities in the night
cities now doomed to die
these things he never saw
but what he saw and did will live as long as we

I am the deconstructed man
my parts are scattered on the nursery floor

and can't be put back together again because the instruction book is lost
clean up your mess in the nursery my mother says
I am the deconstructed man
my older brother laughs at me all the time
he drives me into a rage and I drive the scissors into his knee
he has to have six stitches at the hospital and go on crutches but I pay
      for my jubilation
look mother James is doing it again he's chewing with his
      mouth open
and he hasn't learned his lines of catechism for Sunday
God went back to Heaven when I was twelve, He stopped counting
      the hairs of my head
will he ever come back? I was waiting for Him then but now I'm
      waiting for Godot
Pound said "C'est moi dans la poubelle."
they had to chop us both up to get us into that trashcan in Paris
but why was there no blood? there's never any blood
did Abel bleed? did En Bertrans the sower of discord bleed
there in the bolge holding his severed head by the hair and swinging
      it like a lantern
E'l capo tronco tenea per la chiome
Pesol con mano a guisa di lanterna
E quel mirava noi, e dicea "oh me!!"
(Bos chavaliers fo e bos guerriers . . .
e bos trobaire e savis e be parlans . . .)
why don't I bleed what is it that my heart is pumping?
Cynthia said it was embalming fluid and she went away
like God and mother Cynthia went away
I am the deconstructed man
I do the best I can

Lie quiet Ezra there in your campo santo on San Michele
in paradisum deducant te angeli
to your city of Dioce to Wagadu to your paradiso terrestre
what I have reft from you I stole for love of you
belovèd my master and my friend.

94

"Multas per gentes . . .": *Catullus CI. "By strangers' coasts and waters, many days at sea"* *(Robert Fitzgerald's version). The next line was composed by Fitzgerald in our golf cart in Carolina, on request for how Catullus would deal with airplane travel.*

POLUMETIS: *the Homeric epithet for Odysseus, the man of many counsels.*

"J'ai rêvé dans la grotte . . .": *Gérard de Nerval, "El Desdichado," "I was dreaming in the grotto where the mermaids swim."*

"Voi che sapete . . .": *Cherubino's aria in Mozart's* The Marriage of Figaro.

"in ogne parte . . .": *"in every place where memory leads me." Suggested by the line in Cavalcanti's "Donna mi priegha": "In quelle parte dove sta memoria."*

"A ristorar le pene . . .": *Zerlina's duet in Mozart's* Don Giovanni.

"Ma in Ispagna . . .": *Leporello's patter song in* Don Giovanni.

"risplende ognun sa luce . . .": *"each one gives forth her light which will never die."*

"sola et magna (mater)": *"the one and great mother."*

"ma basta per oggi . . .": *"enough for today's catalog of girls."*

"C'est moi dans la poubelle": *"I'm the one in the ashcan." In the 1960s, after he had become depressed, Pound was in Paris and Beckett took him to a performance of* Endgame.

"E'l capo tronco . . .": *"Certainly I saw, and to this hour I seem to see, a trunk going head-less, even as went the others of that dismal throng, and it held the severed head by the hair, swinging in his hand like a lantern, which looking upon us, said, 'Ah me!'"* *(Pound's translation,* The Spirit of Romance, *p. 45.)*

"Bos chavaliers fo . . .": *"He was a good knight and a good fighter, a good poet and wise and well-spoken." From the* vida *of Bertrand de Born.*

"in paradisum . . .": *"may the angels lead you into paradise."*

LA TRISTESSE

And Pound in his despair in the Army prison camp at Pisa
Wrote, *"Tard, très tard je t'ai connue, la Tristesse."*
And he said that the tears he had caused in his life were
    drowning him.
"Les larmes que j'ai créées m'inondent."

I have been reading some pages in the *Tristia* of Ovid,
Who was exiled to Pontus on the Black Sea, the end of nowhere,
Because he had offended Augustus.
Ovid longs for Rome, for his homeland.
You are my homeland and I seek permission to return to you.

You are the solitary voyager, the bird of lone flight.
I was foolish; I tried to capture you, to bring you down from
    your sky.
I am rightly punished, but exile from you is a hard pain to bear.
My sadness is a dull ache, a wound that won't heal.
I have injured the one I love best.
She also has her wound, the one I gave her.
La tristesse, tard, très tard je t'ai connue.

THE STRANGER

There was a knock at the door; I opened.
It was a young man I couldn't at first recognize.
But when I heard his voice I knew him.
He was myself some thirty years before.

I asked him in and made coffee.
Why did you never write, I thought you were dead?
I wished I was sometimes, he said, better I had been.
Where were you all these years?
What did your old poet say, through many lands
And over many seas, I saw so much.
And what were you doing? He shrugged.
Often I didn't know what I was doing.
You might say I was trying to find out
What was real and what was not.
I did a lot of harm, much of it to myself.

We talked for several hours, then he said he had to go.
I urged him to stay on, told him he could make his home with me.
But he refused. There's much that I still have to do, much to learn.
I may be back and I may not, but it was good to have this time
     with you.
And I'm glad you haven't changed, you're still yourself.

TWO FABLES FROM *THE OCEAN OF STORY*

Story of the Chandala Girl Who Wanted to Marry a Prince

In the city of Chidambaram there was a very pretty
Girl who was determined to marry a prince,
Even though she was a Chandala, the lowest of all the castes.
One day she saw the son of the king who was making a tour of in-
    spection of the city.
She followed his entourage hoping her beauty would catch his eye.
At that moment a holy hermit came by.
The prince got down from his elephant and prostrated himself before
    the *sadhu*.
This showed the girl that a holy man was greater than a prince. She
    followed the *sadhu*.
Soon they reached a temple of Siva, where the holy man knelt and
    worshiped.
The girl made obeisance to the *lingam* and even dared to kiss it.
Then a mongrel dog ran into the temple, sniffed
Around and did as dogs do right on the *lingam*.
Was the dog superior to Siva? How could she wed a dog?
The dog ran into the street and she followed it
To the house of a young Chandala man she knew who was a carter.
The dog leapt up to greet the young man and licked his face.
That settled it, the girl was reconciled to her caste,
And her mother sent for the matchmaker.

Story of the Astrologer Who Killed His Son

There was an astrologer who would stop at nothing to make money.
He left his home province thinking he could do better elsewhere.
There he went about advertising his skill and learning.
He had with him his son who was nine years old.
He embraced his son in the town square and shed tears over him.

When the people questioned him the wicked man told them:
"I know all that is past, and the present,
And what will come in the future.
I can foresee that my child will die in seven days.
That is why I am weeping."
His words aroused the wonder and sympathy of the people.
On the seventh day the astrologer killed
The boy while he was still sleeping.
When the people saw that the prophecy had come true,
They believed in his mastery of the art of prediction.
They honored him with rich gifts.
He acquired much wealth and returned to his own province.

Adapted from the Tawney-Penzer translation of Somadeva's Katha Sarit Sagara
(Sanskrit, 3rd century A.D.).
SADHU: *Sanskrit, ascetic or hermit.*
LINGAM: *Sanskrit, the phallic column in shrines under which Siva
(Shiva) the destroyer-creator god of Hinduism is usually worshiped.*

AN ATTESTATION

I, Enrique Xavier Villaruta, Marqués d'Orizaba
Affirm that the Indian boy known as Miguel Sánchez
Died on my estancia in Córdoba de México
At the age of about sixteen, died of natural causes
And that as witnesseth Fray Escobar of the Franciscans
The marks of the stigmata were found on his body
The five wounds on hands, feet, and the side
And the boy's body has been placed in the tomb
Of my family at the church of San Luis Fernando
Without any embalmment of any kind
Where it has not corrupted or putrified
As observed by many who have come to wonder at it
These six months since the death, uncorrupted
And may the Devil take my soul if I have not truth told
Regarding this miraculous event.

Given by me this 23rd day of February
in the year of our Lord 1534, and in
the reign of the Blessed Felipe of
Aragón, the fifth year
                              Attest: Escobar, O.F.M.
            Villaruta d'Orizaba

THE FLEMISH DOUBLE PORTRAIT

In this painting which hangs in the Hermitage in St. Petersburg
(the artist is unknown but the style is Flemish fifteenth century)
two aristocratic women wearing elegant silk & brocade dresses
are seated facing each other on elaborately carved fauteuils
we see them in profile, they are looking at each other as if engaged
     in conversation
their dresses are similar in cut but one is red and one is green
as we approach the painting we take the ladies to be sisters
on nearer inspection they appear to be twins
but when we look very closely they are indisputably one and the
     same person
the same coiffures, the same beaded slippers, the same gold-chain
     necklaces
a small mole (reversed of course) in the cheeks near the mouth
the ladies are staring at each other with unconcealed hatred
you might say that they are trying to set fire to each other with their
     eyes
their hands are clenched tight in their laps
if you linger before this painting for only a few moments
you may become hypnotized by the enmity it contains (such hatred,
     such hatred)
you may even feel hallucination stealing into your mind
you may imagine that you hear the women hissing at each other (in
     whatever is your language)
one asks, what are you doing inside me that I feel such excruciating
     pain?
and the other replies, it is you who have no right to be in me, I de-
     mand that you go, I never wanted you, I never loved you, go
     now, you must go!

SOME MEMORIES OF E. P. (DRAFTS & FRAGMENTS)

Rapallo (1934)

So I came to Rapallo, I was eighteen then
and you accepted me into your Ezuversity
where there was no tuition, the best beanery since Bologna.
Literachoor, you said, is news that stays news
and quoting from some bloke named Rodolphus Agricola,
"ut doceat ut moveat ut delectet."
You taught me and you moved me and you gave me great delight.
Your conversation was the best show in town,
whatever you'd ever heard or read as fresh as when it first got in your
    head.
The books you loaned me were filled with caustic marginalia.
To keep from losing them you hung your glasses and your pens and
    scissors from strings over your desk.
You read my poems and crossed out half the words, saying I didn't
    need them.
You told me not to bother writing stories because Flaubert and
    Stendhal and James and Joyce had done all that could be done
    with fiction.
They say you were cranky, maybe so, but only with people who de-
    served it,
stupid professors busy killing poetry and international bankers making
    usury and *i mercanti di cannoni* selling arms to both sides of a war.
You elucidated the Mysteries, all about *dromena* and *epopte,* and how it
    was *epopte* that sent the sperm up into a man's brain to make him
    smart.
You loved cats and the cats loved you.
Some days we would walk up the stoney salite on the mountainside
    behind town
through the olive groves and the little peasant farms where the cats
    were perched on the stone walls.

They were waiting for you, they knew you would bring them a
    packet of scraps from the lunch table.

You would call to the cats, "Micci, micci, micci, vieni qua, c'è da
    mangiare."

And one day when we were feeding the cats near San Pantaleone we
    discussed what you would do with your Nobel Prize money
    when you finally got it

and you thought that a chef would be the best thing since you were
    tired of the food at the Albuggero Rapallo.

And when Henghes the sculptor (id est Heinz Winterfeld Klusmann)
    walked all the way down from Hamburg to see you

because he had heard you had known Gaudier, and he arrived half-
    starved,

you fed him and let him sleep in the big dog kennel on the
    terrace (since there were no extra beds in the penthouse
    apartment)

and you took him to the yard of the man who made gravestones
    and got him credit for a block of marble

from which he carved his sitting-down centaur, and you sold it for
    him to Signora Agnelli, the Fiat lady, in Torino.

And that was the beginning of Henghes' good fortune and fame
    (and the drawing for the centaur became the colophon for
    New Directions).

You said I was such a terrible poet I had better become a publisher, a
    profession which you inferred required no talent and only lim-
    ited intelligence.

And after lunch you would stretch out on your bed with your cow-
    boy hat shielding the sea light from the window

with the big Chinese dictionary on a pillow on your stomach

and you stared at the characters, searching for the glyph of meaning
    in the calligraphy.

(And years later the professor asked your daughter to define your
    ideogramic method

and she thought for a moment and replied that you looked deep into
    the characters to find the truth,

which was a properly Confucian answer.)

And Kung said: "Anyone can run to excesses, it is easy to shoot past
    the mark, it is hard to stand fast in the middle."
And as "Deer Bull" ("Dear Old Hugger-scrunch") loved to say in his
    Paterson,
SO BE IT!

Austria (1936)

And one year we left the Sienese to stew in the Marshes
(since the price offered by Bartolomeo was not high enough to make
    it worthwhile to slug them)
and we called on the Princess Maria at Gais to check on the progress
    of her education
(and you remarked that Herr Marker was a man of sound principles
    because he hung his pants on the crucifix)
Then up over the Brenner into the Tyrol, you and I and the Lady,
to call on Herr Unterguggenberger, the mayor of Woergel, to learn
    the facts of how Vienna had
clamped down on the circulation of *Schwungeld.*
And in Salzburg we put up at the Goldene Rose, on the wrong side
    of the river for economy, where there were bedbugs,
and you came close to blows with Professor X of Haavud
who was frantic to become president of that institution
but was hindered by a little problem of concubinage, which is *mal vu*
    in the town where H. James is interred.
He resented your comments on the curriculum of the world's great-
    est university,
and you didn't see eye to eye on literachoor.

You loved the Mozart and the Vivaldi at the festival
but when we went to the *Festspielhaus* to hear *Fidelio* (Toscanini con-
    ducting)
you began to squirm in fifteen minutes and rose up from your seat to
    sing out:
"Well, what can you expect, the man had syphillis?"
And all this was part of my instruction.

"ut doceat . . .": *"let it teach, move, and delight."*

SALITE: *paths.*

"micci . . .": *"kitty, kitty, kitty, come here; here's something to eat."*

PRINCESS MARIA: *Pound's daughter, Mary, was raised by a peasant family in the Italian Tyrol and later married Prince Boris de Rachewiltz.*

SWUNGELD: *stamp script, at one time used by the town of Woergel, but the Vienna central bank suppressed it.*

"WHEN I WAS A BOY WITH NEVER A CRACK IN MY HEART"

I roamed all roads, hungering to find out
What they meant when they spoke of love.
I was holding my heart in my hand,
Offering it to anyone who would take it.

She who was the first was older than I.
She knew men and their ways.
She had suffered from some who threw her away after their amuse-
     ment.
Now she was seeking an innocent
Whom she could shape to her pleasing.

I will not condemn her;
She taught me so much that I had to learn one way or another.
But I soon began to fear her, beautiful and passionate as she was.
I knew she would alter me in ways I didn't want to accept.
It was only a matter of time till she would incise a crack in my heart,
A crack what would not quickly heal.
So I went on my way;
I took to the road again looking for another less demanding.

Title: from Yeats, "The Meditation of the Old Fisherman."

THE RISING MIST AT ARD NA SIDHE

When I awake at dawn, at the *alba,*
A soft mist is rising from Loch Caragh.
Ta ceo bog ag eiri on loch.
It fingers up from the garden through the trees.
It is reaching for Macgillicuddy's Reeks,
The mountains that stand up from the lake.

The scene could be a Japanese scroll painting
Of Lake Biwa and the hills beyond Kyoto.
But this is not Japan, it is Ireland.
I've not been sleeping on a tatami
With the little wooden pillow block under my neck.
Ketsin is not beside me in the room with walls made of paper.

They wrote me with great respect that Ketsin had died;
That was some forty years ago, she had died in childbirth.
(But this is not Japan, it is Killorglin.)
The slight form of Ketsin is not near for me to touch.
Her frightened smile and her almost inaudible voice no longer com-
     pose a person.
She will not have twined flowers into my Western shoelaces.
She will not bring me my wake-up tea.
She will not ask the morning question:
"Are you awake now, my lord?"

ALBA: *Provençal, the dawn.*
"Ta ceo bog . . .": repeats the title in Irish.

CLUTCHES

My father was an expert automobilist
Once in 1902 in a 5-mile race in Frick Park (Pittsburgh)
(There were two men in each car, a driver and a mechanic)
An important wire fractured from vibration and the vehicle came to
    a halt
My father seized the ends of the wire in each hand, allowing the cur-
    rent to pass through his body
The driver cranked up, leapt back to his seat, grasped the guide bar
    (this was before steering wheels),
The engine sputtered, the car darted forward, and the race was won.

Some 28 years later when I had been given a Model A Ford which
    cost $850
My father was displeased with my driving because I couldn't learn
    how to double-clutch
(To double-clutch you must depress the pedal once while you leave
    the gear you are in, then depress it again to enter the gear in
    which you desire to proceed)
The smoothness of transition, with no bumping or grinding,
    achieved by proper double-clutching is the mark, my father ex-
    plained, of the expert driver.

TIME RUNNING BACKWARDS

That afternoon in a hidden room,
The curtains drawn to half darkness,
The only light coming from scenes out of memory,
Illuminating the walls like passages from a film,
Time running backwards.

Three people are reconvened in judgment on their lives.
Three people, two living and one dead.
The one who is dead is still the most powerful.
But it is a gentle and loving power.
Time running backwards.

Where will time lead the two survivors?
Can the love for a dead man heal their wounds?
Can it obliterate error and faults in emotion?
Can it create a new present, and even a future?
A beloved voice counsels them from the past.
Time running backwards.

THE COUNTRY ROAD

In the painting that hangs in our dining room
A country road, a dirt road, is winding up the slope of a
    mountain ridge;
It begins in pastureland and goes up through scattered trees to
    dense woodland.
It is a scene in western Pennsylvania near the farm where we
    went in summer
To get away from the heat of the city.

I say that the road "is winding," not "winds,"
Because, for me, the painting sometimes seems to be still in
    progress,
Though the dear lady who did it has been dead more than
    fifteen years.
Some days, if I'm alone as I pass through the room,
I may notice some very small alteration in the
    composition
As if the artist were still working on it.
A tree may have slightly changed its position in
    the landscape,
Or the farmhouse and barns in the middle distance;
A patch of color in the pasture or the cornfield of the foreground
    may appear different;
The contour of the mountain ridge against the sky has been
    moving.
Even in the direction that the road is taking, its curves are never
    precisely the same.
It's always a sun-filled scene, but the quality of the light may vary.

As my eyes walk that familiar road, where I walked so often
        as a child,
I see things I hadn't detected before,
Little things of no great importance, but I'm
        aware of them.

Oil painting of "The Country Road" was done by Marjorie Phillips in western Pennsylvania about 1940.

HOW DID LAURA TREAT PETRARCH?

The contemporary records are somewhat vague.
They speak of her beauty and her devotion.
The poems to her have romantic imagery,
But they don't get down to the nitty-gritty.
Did she mend his socks? Did she put up
With his tantrums? Did she make copies
Of his poems? Rub balm on his sore neck?
These are important questions for today's poets
As they set about to choose a life's companion.

PETRARCH: *Francesco Petrarca (1304–74), the great Italian poet and humanist of the Renaissance. His sonnets immortalized the anonymous "Madonna Laura," his lifelong inspiration, who may have been the wife of a Provençal nobleman.*

HER HEART

(for Anne Carson)

is a volcano in eruption
many fearless men have perished there
Menippus of Macedonia, Sardonicus of Tyre,
Cyaxeres the Mede, Kartikeya, lord of the Hindu Kush,
their valor aroused admiration
but their fates were sealed
from the moment they laid eyes on her.
It was like the game called "the vizier's choice"
at the court of Aurangzeb.
They were dazzled by her beauty
and lost all power of judgment.
After their pleasure, they slipped
into her fiery crater
and were consumed.

MENIPPUS ET AL.: *fictitious characters.*
AURANGZEB: *17th-century Mogul emperor of India.*
  A tough nut; he gained the throne by defeating
  his three brothers and imprisoning his father, Shah Jahan.

THE SHAMEFUL PROFESSION

For years I tried to conceal from the villagers that I wrote poetry
I didn't want them to know that I was an oddball
I didn't want the young men with beards wearing baseball caps who
    come to the liquor store in their pickups to buy sixpacks to
    know that I was some kind of sissy
I decided it was prudent to buy the *Daily News* instead of the *Times*
    at the drugstore
I burned my poem drafts at home before I took the trash to the
    dump, kids scavenge around there and the old man who does
    the recycling is nosy
I took every precaution

But our town is not an easy place to keep secrets, everybody knows
    everybody and they gossip when they're getting their mail at the
    post office
Things began to come apart
A young man with long hair and a city accent showed up and asked
    in the stores where the poet Laughlin lived
Then a pipe burst and the plumber told people that he saw thousands
    of books stacked in the cellar, some of them in foreign lan-
    guages
Next day the head of the Volunteer Fire Department came, pretend-
    ing to check the wiring
I began to get a bit paranoid; the town trooper is supposed to check
    each rural road once a week but he came up our road past our
    house three days in succession
The ax fell when somehow a reporter for the county paper heard the
    rumors and there was a little item: local poet caught speeding
    twice on 272, Motor Vehicles may suspend license
Much has changed in my life now
Nobody has laughed at me in the street (I'm over six feet weight 245
    and look pretty fit for my age) but they look at me in a funny
    way

I don't go to Apple House our grocery store anymore because a little
    girl with her finger in her nose pointed me out to the check-
    out lady and asked her something; now I get my liquor and sup-
    plies in the next towns and order Honeybaked Hams from Vir-
    ginia by mail

My life is all different now that they know I write poems.
But if they think they can shame me out of it they're very much
    mistaken. I'm not breaking any law
I'll go on with it unless they have me declared a public nuisance and
    have me sent to the Institute
I've heard there is a poor fellow in the Institute who claims he is
    Henry Wordsworth Longfellow. He'll understand and be my
    friend; we can recite to each other if they won't let us have
    paper and pencils.

A FLORILEGIUM

The Purple Clematis

Each day the purple clematis climbs further up the wire beside the
    kitchen door
Green fingers twine around the strands of wire
And soon there is another blossom with a yellow star at its center
Whom are you chasing, I ask the flower
Are you racing the horses of the sun?
Do you imagine that Phaëthon, son of Helios, has time to fall in love
    with you?
Surely you've heard that he is condemned to die every evening
How like a man, she answers, what do I care about the drivers of
    chariots?
I'm only looking for a small crack in this wall
Where I may conceal myself from that ruffian, the north wind Boreas
Who only too soon will be here with his cruel winter.

The Wild Geranium

How like a flower does Chloe gently bend her head
At the approach of wind or rain
Then comes the sun and quickly she's herself again
Not arrogant but confident of her beauty.

Anthea

Anthea greenly creeps the ground
Her tiny flower hardly to be seen against the rocks
But country people know of her healing power
Zeus promised it for her in recompense
When he forced her mother, the sweet nymph Cleomine.

FLORILEGIUM: *a collection of flowers.*

PHAËTHON: *in Greek mythology the son of Helios, the sun, who met his death trying to drive his father's chariot of horses across the sky.*

ANTHEA: *my name for my muse.*

A LADY ASKS ME

(for Sophie Hawkes)

a discerning friend
if I've been reading Marcabru & Bernart de Ventadourn
how did she know or am I quite transparent
a most discerning lady, dompna de cortes dig e-l dous ris.

Marcabru, the friend of Cercamon who taught him to sing trobar
a crusty fellow, rather a sour apple, if we can believe his vida
whom they called the "maldisant" because he spoke ill of love and of
    women in his sirventes
and what sort of a trip was that for a troubadour
maybe he just couldn't cut the mustard and they treated him badly
but the songs are beautiful and full of invention
non amet neguna, ni d'autra non fo ametz
he says that he never loved anyone and never by anyone was loved
I don't believe it, poets will be liars to make a good poem.

And En Bernart was the son of the castle baker, a bright lad who
    learned to sing well
and he pleased the count and his young lady
but when he pleased the lady too much, the count sent him packing
then he pleased the Duchess of Normandy, and she him
but she had to marry Henry of England for political reasons
so the rest of his life he remembered those two ladies
the sorrows of love he knew but also its joys as his cansos tell
cen vetz mor lo jorn de dolor, e reviu de joi autra cen
a hundred times a day I die of my sadness, and then a hundred times
    come to life again with joy
mais val mos mals qu'autre bes, e pois mos mals aitan bosm'es, bos er
    los bes apres l'afan
even my sorrow is better than any seeming good, so that my sorrow
    seems to me a good, but best is the good that comes after my
    sorrow.

I have heard someone walking below me in the cellar and a voice
    talking above me in the attic
there are no young maids spinning now
there are no lads working in the croft
everything is parody, everything is the same and not the same
there were, there are, the times before
but will there be time coming after
don't say it, and it won't happen
but it could happen, anything can happen
such things have happened before
everything is parody, it has all happened before
the old poems echo in my head, the old poets converse with me
my past is an echo of their earlier pasts
is memory only a parody of what really happened?

Tant ai mo cor ple de joya, tot me desnatura
flor blancha vermelh'e grova, me par la frejura, c'ab lo ven et ab la
    ploya, me creis l'aventura
my heart is so full of joy that the nature of everything is changed
white flowers, crimson and gold, become like the cold, for with the
    wind and the rain my happiness keeps growing

An old book of fair language ful of hy sentence is alwey a goode
    thynge to poure.

Title: the opening line of Guido Cavalcanti's "Donna mi priegha" canzone.
MARCARBRU: *one of the twelfth-century troubadors.*
"non amet neguna. . .": from "Dirai vos senes duptansa" of Marcabru, the last line.
BERNART DE VENTADORN: *another twelfth-century troubador.*
"mais val mos mals . . .": from "Non es meravelha s'eu chan" of Bernart de Ventadorn,
    fourth stanza.
"tant ai mo cor . . .": from "Tant ai mo cor ple de joya" of Bernart de Ventadorn.

THE INN AT KIRCHSTETTEN

Notes Penciled in the Margins of a Book of the Dichtungen
of Georg Trakl

How can I thank you B, for your ear, your mind, your affection?
Some afternoons after we had given kisses we would recline against
the hard bolsters in the little inn reading and rewriting my poems.

At first the idea of exchanging caresses with an almost heavenly
being had frightened me. I committed little crimes so you would
postpone this perilous happiness.

No one had told me that it was possible to make love to a voice.

Only someone who has not shared such love will condemn these
writings.

The toy train which brought us to the town was so slow. It stopped
at every hamlet. Farm people got on and off. There was a car for
their animals: lambs, pigs, chickens. When it was very slow we would
become frantic with impatience. We had so little time to be together.

Outside the window of the inn were the streets of the town, its old
houses. But if we watched hard enough the scene would change
into a landscape of fields, trees, a little lake and mountains in the dis-
tance.

Horses went clip-clop down the cobbled street. It was a blessing
there were so few autos and motorbikes.

There was a gilt-framed mirror on the wall of the room. Why did
we see in it the reflection of only one person?

You were disgusted by the big cockroaches that scuttled across the
floor until I convinced you they carried secret messages. Our post-
men.

I always brought flowers to talk when love had rendered us silent.

Sometimes you would say, I can't remember who we are. I have to look at the shoes on the carpet to recall our names.

A strange ballet. The horizontal pas de deux. Hands mimicking the dancers' feet. Your long hair is your costume?

A bird struck the window with a thud and fell into the street. It was eager to join us but couldn't see the glass.

We read no more that day. There was nothing the book could tell us. Paolo and Francesca, you said. We often heard faint footsteps in the hall, not as heavy as those of the inn servants. You said it was the revenants who wanted to be with us. You opened the door but no one was there.

The inn servants seemed an honest lot but it was just as well to tip them a bit too much. I used the name Reseguier but you might have been recognized from your pictures in the magazines.

There were porcelain basins and pitchers, two of each, on the stand and eider puffs on the bed, two fat white pancakes on the matrimonial.

There was a picture on the wall which I couldn't place, most unusual for a village inn, not a religious or hunting scene. It was an abstract drawing in several colors. A grid of little nearly identical shapes connected by ink lines. Perhaps an artist from the city hadn't been able to pay his bill.

Sometimes, if you dozed, I would change the time on your watch that you always put on the bedside stand. I knew you would wake with a start and say it was time to go home, he would be waiting for your company at tea. There were later trains on the toy railroad.

Hot and cold weather, we went there for nearly a year. Who is using that room now? Perhaps a series of lonely traveling salesmen.

You must know that none of these things may ever have happened, that we imagined them. . . . How can we be sure it was not all an illusion? Remember the wineglass you dropped and it shattered? We tried to get up all the crumbs of glass but some were too small and worked their way into the fabric of the carpet. They would prove we were there.

EDITOR'S NOTE: *The book of Trakl was found in 1983 in a secondhand shop near the Ste-fanskirche in Vienna. The marginal markings, which are written vertically, are in two hands, one male, one female. The neat male hand is in the old German handschrift. The female hand is more difficult to read, a mixture of Romanic and Cyrillic letters. Perhaps from Moldavia?*

Neither B nor her lover has been identified. The bookseller in Vienna could not recall where the Trakl had come from. From the description of the "toy train" the town may have been Kirchstetten, where W. H. Auden was later to have his summer home, and the inn the Drei Falken.

I'M WALKING VERY SLOWLY TODAY

Outside and even in the house
It's such a beautiful day.
I want to make it last.
It snowed in the night, there is no wind,
And the snow is clinging to every branch
Of the trees. Hundreds of tiny white branches
Reaching, but for what? Don't they know
They'll be melted and gone in a few hours?
Even now the sun has come out
With an almost violent brightness.
The snow on the trees is turning
To particles of glistening ice.
Such a shining, a cold radiance.
In a few hours the trees will be bare again,
With the snow under them roughened
Where the ice buds fell into it.

I've been walking as slowly as possible,
Outside as I go to the barn to feed the sheep
And inside as I hunt for the books
I need for something I'm writing.
The brilliance of light pours in
Through the windows. I move very slowly.
I don't want this snow-light to end.
I'd like to stretch it out endlessly.
I'm eighty and I want more such days,
But I know I'm not likely to be given them.

THE SULTAN'S JUSTICE

The mistress of the brothel can neither read nor write   she keeps accounts for the girls with marks on the wall   and that was the year when the Zamindar of Holi accused the little Abyssinian (she was only twelve) of taking a goldpiece from his purse while he was sleeping after his pleasure and she was taken before the Sultan and the mistress (God knows why she was the darling of the place) bore false witness against her   and her right hand was lopped off with the sword according to the law   but later the money was found in the cook's palette and he was punished in the same fashion   so much for the law and the Sultan's justice   it is a serpent that coils around us and we are helpless against its poison.

MAKING A LOVE POEM

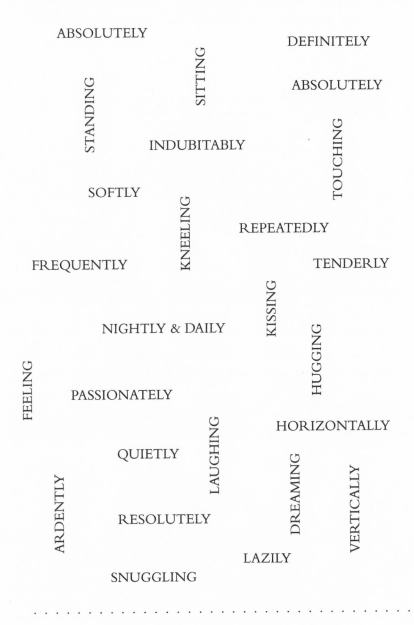

Paolo & Francesca Should Make Love Again

WHAT THE OLD BEDOUIN TOLD ME

Once in my long ago
there was so much rain
that many of the animals died
the leaves and grasses
could not come up to feed them.

And once in my long ago
there were sounds more frightening than thunder
I fell when the earth fell, moving under my feet
part of the mountains fell into the desert
and the sea invaded the land.

And once in my long ago
the sun came too close to the earth
each day nearer and nearer
a dislocation of the heavenly order
first the lakes dried up, then the streams, then the springs
only the glacier people in the mountains survived.

In my long ago I have known these abominations
against nature, these deadly marvels.

*In Arabic there is no exact equivalent for our word "history." A Bedouin might say
"in my long ago."*

A LEAVE-TAKING

(for Robert Fitzgerald)

My old friend has departed, he is making the inevitable journey
Not, I think, to dark Erebus, but to a happier place
Reserved for the good & the great, for our friends the Greek & Latin
　　poets.
And I believe that such a land exists though I am uncertain of its lo-
　　cation
Because, idiotic as they are, the gods must have provided it for such as
　　he.

Memory must be my comforter, he gave so much to remember
As when one night long ago we sat on the roof of Dunster House
Watching the stars pursue their courses
And he related to me much wisdom from the philosophers
And no doubt I related to him frivolities about young female persons.
We reflected on the human condition
And reviewed the lives of our heroes, we spoke of the sorrows of
　　poets
How those girls made Catullus so miserable, how Ezra drifted into ir-
　　reality
How François got himself strung on the gallows, and Kleist dis-
　　patched himself and Henriette with two bullets.

But we did not jump off the roof of Dunster House, though nothing
　　would have been easier
Because there were things we both had to do with the lives the gods
　　had entrusted to us, such as
the fashioning of words into poems and sentences.
And later we did those things according to our powers, his great and
　　mine small
But each of us found joy in the doing—and in the bond which en-
　　dured between us.

BUILDING 520, BELLEVUE

Building 520 at Bellevue is a temple

It is a shrine to Thanatos, the personification of death, marble and
glass and aluminum with a long inscription on the wall of the
atrium in somewhat cockeyed Latin

Which tells us that this is a joyous place, a hortulus memoriarum, a
garden of fond memories, quis risum non excludet, where
laughter is not banished

There is soft Muzak, Schubert's "Ave Maria" and "Humoresque"
while I was there

The dignified male receptionist in a slightly Renaissance uniform di-
rected me respectfully to the office of Miss Bland

Miss Bland is loveliness itself, wearing a dress of cheerful, sunny silk

She has been trained, I think, in ballet as well as psychology; she
speaks softly in an accent of either Bryn Mawr or Radcliffe

The drapes of her office match the color of her frock

A most courteous young lady who writes rapidly in a nice script, the
very model of a modern civil servant

"Ah yes," she says, glancing at her computerized list, "you are visiting
Number 29, who came to us yesterday morning."

A few more particulars, and then, almost apologetically, "Is there any-
thing you can tell me, this is for our statistical records, anything
about Number 29's last moments, that is the method of his de-
cease?"

I told her what little I cared to tell her. "Ah yes," she said with a small
sigh, "a kitchen knife," and she wrote that down

Then she pressed a button on her intercom, "May we have Number
29?" She said, "If you'll just take a seat for a moment."

It became a longer and longer moment, then I heard her, quite angry,
on her intercom, "Damn it, Harry, what are you doing with
Number 29 down there?"

She led me through her office to another room, where a sign on the
door said "Viewing Room," a small room where one wall was a

plate-glass window, the whole room bathed in a soft glow from hidden lights

Here the Muzak was different, it was I think a Richard Rodgers arrangement of "Jesu Joy of Man's Desiring," but very soft

There were comfortable chairs for those who might need them "Shall we?" asked Miss Bland, and when I nodded she pressed a button beside the window

Number 29 rose slowly from below as if unseen arms were raising him on an open palanquin, very slowly he came up from below

He was entirely covered, except for his face and some of his hair, in a kind of cape, its material of an off-white color, which was like a vestment

He resembled one of Manzù's sculptures of a cardinal stretched out on his bier

And he had now the long, thin face of his ancestors because there was no blood left in him

I spoke silently, to that silent form, saying "I pray you will have a good crossing."

And perhaps I only imagined that he answered, "Thanks Dad, thanks for coming. I'll miss you. Thanks for everything."

Miss Bland said, very gently, "Is that he?" I told her that was he

When I signed the form she took me out into the light of day.

DYLAN

One of us had to make the official identification of Dylan's body at
    the Medical Examiner's Morgue
Brinnin and I tossed a coin and I lost
It was a crummy building in the hospital complex on First Avenue
    and the basement, smelling of formaldehyde, was a
    confusion of trolleys with rubber sheets covering bodies
A little old man in a rubber apron was in charge
He put on his glasses to read the name I had written on a slip of
    paper and looked around, trying to remember
He lifted one sheet. "Is this him?" It wasn't
Two or three more who weren't "Old Messy" of the pubs of Soho
    and Chelsea
Finally we found him and he looked awful, all bloated
"Insult to the brain" was what it said on the autopsy report, too
    much booze for too many years
The old man sent me to a window to confirm the identification
    where there was a little girl about five feet high, struggling
    with the forms, using a pencil stub
She got me to write "Dylan" for her on the
    form because she had never heard of
    such a name and couldn't spell it
"What was his profession?" she asked
I told her he was a poet; she looked perplexed
"What's a poet?" she asked
I told her a poet was a person who wrote poems
She put that down, and that's what it says
    on the form:
Dylan Thomas—a poet (he wrote poems).

1953

130

BOOK IV

(AMERICAN) FRENCH POEMS

L'ARRIVÉE DU PRINTEMPS

Je pense à toi mon coeur
est rempli de ton être

tu cours dans mes veines
comme la sève du printemps

tu es toujours loin mais
même ici je sens ta touche

douce comme la bise méridi-
onale ne tards pas de venir

Persephone ne tards pas je
t'attends avec impatience.

LA LUCIOLE

Je te vois voltigeante dans la
nuit et je te poursuis pour t'at-

traper   tu es presqu'insaisissable
mais à la fin je te tiens   mais

quand j'ouvre la main tu n'es
pas là   tu m'as échappé de nou-

veau   qu'est-ce que tu chasses
c'est clair que ce n'est pas

moi   je plains la vélocité de
tes alternances affectives

mais je ne sais pas si je veux
te faire changer car si tu é-

tais toujours prévisible serais
tu rasante comme les autres?

THE FIREFLY

I see you flashing in the night and try to catch you
But it's almost impossible to seize you
When I open my hand you're not there, you've escaped me again
What are you hunting for?
It's clear that it's not me
I begrudge the speed of your changes of affection
But I don't think I'd want to change you
If you were always predictable
Might you not become as boring as the others?

J'IGNORE OÙ ELLE VAGUE
CE SOIR

quelqu'un l'a vue à Ecbatan
et un autre à Samarkande   le

monde est grand et plein de
séductions pour une belle

fille   mais je lui enverrai
par pigeon voyageur ce mot

qu'il y aura toujours pour
elle un logement à l'abri

ici dans mon coeur fidèle.

I DON'T KNOW WHERE SHE IS
WANDERING TONIGHT

Someone saw her in Ecbatan
And another in Samarkand
The world is wide and full of seductions
For a beautiful girl
But I'll send her this word by carrier pigeon
That for her there will always be lodging and shelter
Here in my faithful heart.

MON SECRET

Je demande qu'on me donne
un lit à l'hôpital des fous

figurez-vous comme j'ai souf-
fert dans ce beau monde tel

qu'il est   mon nom n'est pas
vraiment celui qui est in-

scrit sur ma carte d'identi-
té   personne ne sait qui je

suis (et je ne vais pas vous
le dire   c'est mon secret à

moi) j'attends de rencontrer
le Bon Dieu à l'hôpital des

fous   à Lui j'avouerai mon
vrai nom   il me reconnaîtra et

arrangera tout pour mon bien.

MY SECRET

I demand that they give me a bed
in the insane asylum
Just imagine how I've suffered in
this "beautiful world" the way it is
My name is not really what's
inscribed on my identity card
Nobody knows who I am
(and I'm not going to tell you)
It's my secret
I expect to meet God in the asylum
I'll tell Him my real name
He will recognize me
And arrange things for my welfare.

ELLE N'EST PLUS NOCTAMBULE

Elle ne vient plus me rendre visite
dans mes rêves qui sont maintenant

cavernes solitaires et ténébreuses
où vraiment est-elle   dans sa derni-

ère lettre elle m'a ècrit qu'elle al-
lait vers le source du Nil pour re-

trouver le Prêtre Jean   que c'était lui
et pas moi le prince qu'elle atten-

dait   que dois-je croire   on sait bien
que le Prêtre Jean n'existe pas   per-

sonne dans tous les siècles n'a jamais
dècouvert son royaume d'ivoire

et d'or   et moi est-ce que moi-même
j'existe   quand elle est si lointaine

je n'en suis pas certain.

SHE WALKS NO LONGER IN THE NIGHT

She doesn't come anymore to visit me in my dreams
Which are now solitary and shadowy caverns
Where is she really?
In her last letter she wrote me
That she was going to the source of the Nile to find Prester John
That he was the prince she was waiting for
What must I think?
Everyone knows that Prester John never existed
In all the centuries no one had discovered his kingdom of ivory
     and gold
And I, do I myself exist?
When she is far away I cannot be certain.

PRESTER JOHN: *legendary Christian priest and king who ruled over a vast, wealthy empire in either Asia or Africa.*

LA GOMME À EFFACER

On dit que c'ést Dieu qui
tient la gomme à effacer

et nous lisons dans la
Bible qu'il se préoccupe de

nous   mais si cela est vrai
pourquoi est-ce qu'il ne'ef-

face pas ma mémoire l'i-
mage dorlotée de toi qui ne

me quitte ni jour ni nuit.

THE ERASER

They say that the power of erasure in our lives belongs to God
And we read in the Bible that he is concerned about us
But if that is true
Why does he not erase from my memory
The adorable image of you
Which will not leave me night or day?

LES CONSOLATIONS

Les trésors de la vieillesse
Sont les petites aventures
de l'imagination.
Un beau visage fait revenir
          un autre
Qu'on a bien aimé loin dans
          le passé.
Alors on se console en disant
"De nouveau je suis jeune."

THE CONSOLATIONS

The treasures of old age
Are the little adventures
      of the imagination.
A beautiful face recalls
      another
That was so much loved
      long ago.
And we console ourselves
Saying, "I'm young again."

BOOK V

SOME PEOPLE THINK

that poetry should be a-
dorned or complicated I'm

not so sure I think I'll
take the simple statement

in plain speech compress-
ed to brevity I think that

will do all I want to do.

TECHNICAL NOTES

Catullus is my master and I mix
a little acid and a bit of honey
     in his bowl love

is my subject & the lack of love
which lack is what makes evil a
     poet must strike

Catullus could rub words so hard
together their friction burned a
     heat that warms

us now 2000 years away I roll the
words around my mouth & count the
     letters in each

line thus eye and ear contend in-
side the poem and draw its move-
     ment tight Milton

thought rhyme was vulgar I agree
yet sometimes if it's hidden in
     the line a rhyme

will richen tone the thing I most
despise is quote poetic unquote
     diction I prefer

to build with plain brown bricks
of common talk American talk then
     set 1 Roman stone

among them for a key I know Ca-
tullus knew a poem is like a blow
    an impact strik-

ing where you least expect this I
believe and yet with me a poem
    is finally just
    a natural thing.

POETS ON STILTS

Writing on stilts is in vogue
these days. The taller the stilts
the easier to be in fashion.
Very few poets now want to walk
with their feet on the ground,
they might get their shoes wet.

These poets buy their stilts
at some beanery. Stilts from a
creative writing course are
especially prized. Such stilts
are the tallest.

Stilts can give a superior view
of almost anything the poet
wants to write about. Altitude
makes the poet feel important
and it gets him into the club.

But a word of warning to
stiltwalkers. The higher they
fall from their stilts, the
bigger the smash when they
hit the pavement.

THEN AND NOW

The Rain

is speaking it pelts
against the windows
and on the roof
in the night
it makes thousands
of little words
which confuse the child
who does not understand
such a language
what is the rain
trying to tell him
should he be afraid
is there a message
of danger to be escaped
or can he be lulled
by the sound of the rain
and go back to sleep?

The Poem

is moving by itself
it proceeds of its
own accord
the writer of the poem
has no idea where
it will lead him
he cannot control it
because it has
its own life
separate from his own
what if it carries him off
from his safe life
from his accustomed loves
should he fear harm
from the poem and tear up
the page or simply put it
aside and go back to sleep?

THE UNANSWERABLE
QUESTION

It's easy to oblige you
when you say your whole

body wishes to be touching
all of mine from forehead

to feet   but what of the
soul   how can we realize

the soul   what is its lo–
cus   where does it reside?

*The last two lines echo the language of Pound's Cavalcanti
translations.*

WILL WE EVER GO TO
THE LIGHTHOUSE?

We see it every day from
the shore and we talk of

sailing out on a happy ex-
pedition we will carry our

gifts to the lighthouse-
keepers but the weather

is always poor or the wind
is wrong and year by year

the lighthouse appears to
become more distant from

us until we are no longer
certain it is really there.

SILENTIUM AUREATUM EST

If I give you some of my silence
will you give me some of yours

there's something important that
most people aren't aware of be-

cause they're too busy being busy
silence is nourishing it's good

to eat   it's the opposite of hun-
ger which is a paining emptiness

silence (especially if it can be
shared) is a satisfying fullness

Carthusian monks and the Trap-
pists live by silence   animals

rely on silence for their safety
and for us humans silence can be

a garment of warmth & protection.

THE MOUNTAIN AFTERGLOW

Afterglow goldens the
peak its rock beak glows

like raw blood and red
red is the snowfield

beneath it inevitably my
thoughts go to Christ's

blood which our weakness
drinks and to the blood

of another useless hope-
less war then from its

blackness the heart cries
to the peak O give us a

sign make us a sign
but back to our valley

comes only the sun's
dying glow as so softly

so delicately the bright
rock and snow fade into

night and night clouds
fold dark on the stars.

The Wasatch Mountains at Alta, Utah.

A NIGHT OF RAGAS

Those all-night concerts in India
that began at dusk and went on till
nearly dawn. In the open, the audience
squatting on the ground. A platform
for the performers. The singer, usually
suggesting the melody and a soft
tabla, played with the hands, giving
the rhythm. The songs were the love
ragas of of Krishna and Radha. The god
and the cow-herding girl he loved:

> Let the earth of my body be mixed
> with the earth my beloved walks on.
> Let the fire of my body be the brightness
> in the mirror that reflects his face.
> Let the water of my body join the waters
> of the lotus pool he bathes in.

Till I learned that the scale of Vedic
music is different than ours, sometimes I
thought a woman's voice was flat; it was
dropping eighth tones, but when I got
used to the scheme of it, the singing
became very compelling. It moved me
deeply. I can hear it still and see
the scene, the audience silent in its
appreciation of the artistry. The
shadows over the crowd lit up by
flaming lamps on the sides of the
square and over the performers'
platform.

"Let the earth of my body . . .": Denise Levertov's translation in In
Praise of Krishna.

ALL THE CLOCKS

in the house have stopped running.
They've quit moving their hands
at different times. It's very confusing.
The kitchen clock stopped at 6:35.
The grandfather clock, that has to be
would with a key, gave up at 10:15,
and the key won't turn in it now.
The alarm clock by my bed is mute
at 4:30. How did I manage when I was
a child and couldn't tell time?
I went by light and dark. And whether
I was hungry. That will have to
do me till the clocks end
their strike. Or will the strike
spread to other houses? I must
call up the neighbors to see
whether their clocks have given
up too and what they are doing
about it. This situation is a
nuisance but, honestly, I don't
really blame the clocks. Can you
imagine what it's been like for
them? Minutes, hours, days, weeks,
months, years plodding around
the same circular treadmills,
being taken for granted, no thanks
to them from anybody. This could
stop the world. If we get them out
of this somehow and history goes
on, will historians write about
the revolution of the clocks?

THE SECRET ROOM

People forget (if they ever knew it)
That they hear their own voices
Not through their ears
But in their own throats
Is there an image as well
For every breath of sound?

Yes, there's an image
But it seldom can be seen.
It moves too rapidly
And does not linger,
It escapes the eye.

Yet nothing, sound or sight
Is entirely lost—every sensation
Every face or voice
Is stored in the hidden room.
At the back of the brain
Only the keeper of dreams
Has the key to that hidden room.

IS WHAT WE EAT

an indication of what we
are or of what we'd like

to be Rimbaud wanted to
eat the air and Jarry the

noise of grasshoppers hav-
ing lived in India & Jap-

an it is hard for me to
swallow any more rice Pe-

tronius relates that the
guests at Trimalchio's

dinner put their fingers
down their throats to en-

joy a second meal & Rabe-
lais made Gargantua a

ridiculous figure (some
men like to eat pussy but

that is another story) the
mouth eats and the mouth

speaks it's more than a
paradox it's a dilemma

and no doubt people on
food stamps take a more

serious view of eating.

ABOVE THE CITY

You know our office on the 18th
floor of the Salmon Tower looks
          right out on the

Empire State and it just happened
we were there finishing up some
          late invoices on

a new book that Saturday morning
when a bomber roared through the
          mist and crashed

flames poured from the windows
into the drifting clouds and sirens
          screamed down in

the streets below it was unearthly
but you know the strangest thing
          we realized that

none of us were much surprised be-
cause we'd always known that those
          two paragons of

progress sooner or later would per-
form before our eyes this demon-
          stration of their
          true relationship.

IT'S MARCH

and the sap is running in
the sugar maples   the chil-

dren from the brotherhood
are collecting the sap buck-

ets in our woodlot   it's an
outing for them and they're

laughing and shouting most
merrily   there's still a

foot of snow so it's hard
going for some of the lit-

tle ones to drag the buck-
ets to the tank wagon with-

out spilling them   the old
horse who pulls the wagon

droops his head he's bored
he longs to get back to the

stable for his feed   the chil-
dren from the brotherhood wear

old-fashioned clothes but in
bright colors mostly blues &

reds it's a scene from Brueghel.

THE MOTHS

Remembering Vladimir Nabokov

A dark damp night and a sudden hatch
of moths has covered the glass of the

big window in the living room   attract-
ed by the light where I sit reading

they make a solid curtain of flutter-
ing little shapes   they are desperate

they are the kind which only lives for
one night and they must reach the light

there must be thousands of them   there
is nothing remarkable in this invasion

no metaphor for the poet to play with
but now again it is a night some forty

years ago   the summer when Volya came
to hunt lepidoptera at the mountain

lodge in Utah   he had turned the inside
lights against the picture window and

the outside was swarming with moths
he put on a miner's headlamp and stood

on a stepladder on the terrace plucking
the moths into a cyanide jar with his

tweezers   next morning when he examin-
ed the bodies with a jeweler's ocular

he was ecstatic   eleven of the male
moths were the variants (detectable by

a mutation in the genitalia) which were
first recorded by the French lepidopter-

ologist D'Imbert when he visited the
Wasatch range in 1896   later Volya told

me that he traded his duplicates with
collectors in Europe for rarities from

Manchuria & Tibet that he had never seen.

SO MUCH DEPENDS

(for William Carlos Williams)

Bill on the way you saw
the way your heart saw

what your eyes saw not
just the way you saw a

wheelbarrow or the falls
or the blossoms of the

shad tree or Floss in a
rose and 100 other flow-

ers your patients & the
babies and the measure

of your lines in Brueg-
hel's painting of that

dance so many things the
rest of us would never

have seen except for you.

THE BEAUTIFUL MUTTERING

The young man who becomes an old man
as we read his Cantos is telling us

all he knows about everything he has
ever done or seen or heard or read

his discourse is like the endless
beating of the surf on the shore

the poluphloisboio thalasses of
Homer it is the voice of the blind

singer and the voice of the old man
in the village square near Chindam-

baram who is intoning the Ramayana
again and again and again it is an al-

most interminable muttering but of
such grace of phrase of such wisdom

that we are lost in its spell we
want to live for ourselves every-

thing the poet has done or seen
or heard or read *sic scriptum est.*

SOME OF US COME TO LIVE

inside his Cantos like a pal-
ace ten times larger than Ver-

sailles so many rooms so many
corridors the phalanx of par-

ticulars and those long gal-
leries with their endless vis-

tas of a past that no one else
has seen so well or understood

so well the mirrors that re-
flect into each other making

the rhymes between ideas yes
it is the father's house of

many mansions with its place
for each of us places for all.

(for Ezra Pound)

A CERTAIN IMPERMEABLE
PERSON

is quite impossible to describe
with accuracy but let me jot down

a few random notes about her (char-
acteristics that I have now and then

observed)   first when it rains she
doesn't melt   second by powers of

concentration alone she is able in
an instant to change the color of

her hair   thirdly when she walks
past Southwark Cathedral those an-

cient bells ring out in salutation
untouched by the sexton's hand

if you will imagine a female Rim-
baud it is she (but without his

questionable habits)   don't smile
I swear there really is such a

person impermeable impenetrable
and immutable oh I know her well.

(for Vanessa)

THE GODDESS

I have seen the goddess
with my mortal eyes they

were filming down the
street and it was Meryl

Streep she was attended
by five trailers eight

trucks thirty technici-
ans and four policemen

the whole street was il-
lumined with a heavenly

blaze she walked up the
steps of the house four

times and I know that she
saw me and smiled at me

she knew that I was her
devotee she went into

the house but they said
the next scene was in-

side and I couldn't go
in will I ever see her

again my goddess but it
doesn't really matter I

saw her and she knew me.

MARTHA GRAHAM

Earth and water air
and fire her body

beats the ground it
flows it floats it

seems to burn she
burns herself away

until there is no
body there at all

but only the pure
elements moving as

music moves moving
from her into us.

THE CALENDAR OF FAME

"Farewell, farewell, my beloved hands"
Said Rachmaninoff on his deathbed:
And Joseph Hofmann, the great pianist,
Invented the windshield wiper
From watching his metronome.
Genius that I am, all I can do
Is hit wrong keys on my typewriter.

AGATHA

has now gone up to Harlem
to look for a Black Prince

she has exhausted midtown
and lower Manhattan   she

is the daughter of the Rev-
erend Theophilus Gant rec-

tor of Christ Church Newbury
her mother died young and he

repressed her childhood.

THE TIME STEALER

She bites off chunks of time
and hides them   at first she

was concealing them around the
house and I was able to get a

lot of them back but now she's
burying them out in the veg gar-

den where they're hard to find
you have your own time I tell

her why can't you make do with
that   I need all my time   I have

important work to do   she says
if you were a good husband you'd

understand that my time
is your time and your time is

my time   I know she's right but
you can't teach an old dog new

tricks   I'm a crusty self-cen-
tered cantankerous old buzzard

and I wish she'd quit stealing
so many big chunks of my time.

IL PASTOR FIDO

Son' io il pazzo assurdo
che ti vuole troppo bene

al' stesso momento sento
brama e paura il tremor

d'amore mi dà gioia ed
angoscia perchè ho fatto

ciò che Iddio interdice
mi sono guardato nelle

fonte ma era il tuo vi-
so che ho visto là una

beltà riservata agli immor-
tali d'Olimpo non sono

che un pastore campestre
la mia pena è grave saró

sempre pazzo ma sono con-
tento perchè quando ti

guardavo nell' acqua mi sono
convinto che tu sorridevi.

The history of this poem is curious but very sad. In the liceo of the town of Chieti near Pescara there was a 14-year-old student named Egidio Bacigalupo. He had become infatuated with Pulcheria, the beauty of the class. But she scorned him. The class had been studying Guarini's masterpiece of the pastoral genre Il Pastor Fido ("The Faithful Shepherd"). Hoping to heighten her esteem for him, Egidio wrote this poem in imitation of Guarini and slipped it into Pulcheria's desk. But when she found it she gave it to the teacher. The teacher read the poem aloud, ridiculing its content and metric. That night Egidio went out into the darkness and drowned himself in the village duckpond. The case received consider-able notice in the press, and this translation of the poem was published in the Rome Daily American *for 16 June 1963.*

> I am the absurd lunatic
> Who loves you too much
> In the same moment I feel longing and fear
> The tremor of love gives me both joy and anguish
> Because I have done something the gods forbid
> I looked at myself in the fountain pool
> But it was your face I saw there
> A beauty reserved for the immortals on Olympus
> I am only a rustic shepherd
> My punishment will be severe
> I'll always be mad but I am content
> When I saw you in the water
> I knew you were smiling at me

HER LETTERS

Did he imagine that her letters
were written to him those ones

which described in such detail
the topography of her heart (though

always in phrases whose chaleur
did not exceed what was permis-

sible to a lady of breeding and
discretion) didn't he know she

was writing to someone who did
not exist or at least no longer

existed for her because she was
tired of him oh so bored with

him but didn't know how to break
off   and so he had become a phan-

tom it being her disposition to
write to a lover alive or dead.

*Elle n'en continuait pas moins à lui érire des lettres amoureuses, en vertu de cette idée
qu'une femme doit toujours écrire à son amant.*
*Mais, en écrivant, elle percevait un autre homme, un fantôme fait de ses plus ardents sou-
venirs. . . .*

—EMMA'S LETTERS TO LÉON
Madame Bovary

LOSING BODY HEAT

You know how when it gets cold
in the night sometimes you'll

lie there (still half asleep)
without the energy to get up

to find another blanket you'll
stay there till you're nearly

freezing   it was like that for
them for quite a time after they

had been married about five years
they both knew it wasn't working

out but neither could do or say
anything to stop the drift   it

was as if they were paralyzed
they'd lost all their body heat.

THE MERCY IN IT

An old man gone weak in the legs,
Who once danced the hours away,
Must now be content with his books
And what the poets say.

Let him sit in his chair in the sun
And watch how his flowers are growing,
There muse on the past
And on truths that are still worth knowing.

Let him walk with his cane by the lake,
Where the water so slowly moves,
Hearing talk in the clouds
That tells of his heart's old loves.

Parody of Yeats.

PROGNOSIS

An old man alone in a house
full of books who spits in

the sink where he piles his
lonely dishes the children

have gone to make their own
mistakes and he climbs on

the books like an endless
endless ladder grasping at

Dante clutching at Lao Tze
defying the world of things

and lost in a world of words
an old man who stares at

the page till the words are
gone and he knows that he

doesn't even understand
what makes the weather.

WITH MY THIRD EYE

I see what's past and what's
to come I see you as a little

girl you wore your hair in
pigtails then telling the

other children what was right
and what was wrong & then I

watch you in your ashram time
wearing your saffron robe your

head now shaved telling those
other nuns what's right what's

wrong this is your karma this
your destiny prostrate your-

self a thousand times and say
the prayer om mani padme hum.

IT DOES ME GOOD

to bow my body to the ground
when the emperor passes I am

one of the gardeners at the
palace but I have never seen

his face when he walks in the
garden he is preceded by boys

who ring little bells and I
bow myself down when I hear

the bells approaching though
they say that the emperor is

very kind and not easily of-
fended he might smile at me

if I look up or even speak
to me but I believe that the

emperor rules by my humility
it is my humility that rules.

THE WOOD NYMPH

(for Erica)

Sometimes when I am working
In the forest clearing brush from
The hemlocks, a wood nymph approaches
Walking her two small dogs.
Soft-footed and undulant she glides
Through the trees, a figure of grace,
A nymph of surpassing beauty.
Sometimes in her passage she'll stop
To greet me. *Xaire,* she says, *xaire*
Broté; greeting to you, mortal man.
Clear-voiced, she speaks as if
She were singing. She tells of
The spirits that inhabit the marshes.
She is the guardian of those who
Live in bogs and wetlands.
She never identifies herself
But I think she may be Melissa
of Kalymnos, the child of Athena
By a mortal named Euclidon; she
Was renowned for her singing.

MELISSA AND EUCLIDON: *fictitious characters.*

THE TROUT

A trout let us say
a blue blonde trout

that slips through
the bars like water

from boite to boite
from man to man but

only ones she likes
and almost never for

money and I love she
says I love exagger-

ate and her mother
asked the neighbors

qu'est-ce que j'ai
fait au ciel pour

avoir une fille qui
est de l'ordure and

she came back from
the palaces of the

king's cousin out in
Siam where they ate

off gold plates and her
whim was his com-

mand came back to the
bars and the boys and

the slow swim through
the dim light yes a

trout let us call her
a small blonde trout.

THE THINKING MACHINE

I love my neural network
because it talks like me

but if I question its un-
derstanding of what I'm

saying it gets very angry
its inventor claims that

within ten years it will
be knowing things that no

mortal mind has ever con-
ceived of   it does not

have to rest and it runs
all night evaluating by

its binary process the
sentences it has been

given to digest   already
it has assimilated some

Latin phrases but when
I fed it Williams's *ni-*

hil in intellectu quod
non prius in sensu (no

ideas but in things) a
concept which it should

have liked it was puz-
zled and became irrita-

ble because its language
can now only be concrete.

In a California laboratory a computer is being programmed to think like a human. The technical name of the machine is "a neural network," but in the lab its familiar name is "Psych."

PENELOPE VENIT ABIT HELENE

It was raining during her lunch
hour and to keep dry she went
into one of those shabby little
theatres near Times Square.
In the next seat was a well-
dressed benevolent looking
gentleman perhaps in his sixties.
Because he resembled her father
back in Des Moines she did not
feel frightened when he took
her hand and drew it to his
waist. Such a nice old man.
                    (*after Martial*, Ep 1.62)

*Update of a famous poem by Martial. A noble Roman lady goes to
    the baths at Baiae, which were notorious for loose morals. She
    enters the place as virtuous as Penelope, the wife of Ulysses, but
    leaves it a slut like Helen of Troy.*

WHY

when you put your legs up
against the wall after we

had made love did I think
of Nerval's tour abolie a

very strange and dubious
connection your legs are

lithe & lovely and the
tower is presumably if

anyone ever found it a
gothic ruin the way the

mind works is a puzzle
could it be that the mu-

sic of the poem came back
to me when you made that

so graceful and spontane-
ous movement of a dancer.

NERVAL: *Gérard ne Nerval (1808–55), French romantic writer. The poem is "El Desdichado." It tells of "le Prince d'Aquitaine à la tour abolie." The line appealed to T. S. Eliot and is quoted on the last page of* The Waste Land.

ROME: IN THE CAFÉ

She comes at eleven every morning
to meet a man who makes her cry

they sit at a table in the back row
talking very earnestly and soon

she begins to cry   he holds her
hand and reasons with her & she

tries to smile when he leaves
her   then she cries again and

orders a brandy and gulps it
down   then she makes her face

new and goes home   yes I think
that she knows that I come just

to watch her & wait for the day
when he does not come at all.

THE SONGBIRD

The mad contralto in room 503
of the Hôtel des Illusions has

begun her scales   she is con-
siderate of the other guests

and only sings between 11 & 3
when most of them are out   they

are not scales such as you might
hear in a music school   she makes

them up differently each day
she seldom leaves her room so

I haven't met her   perhaps she
is German (I'm not sure) but I've

heard sequences of notes that re-
minded me of *Parsifal* or *Wozzeck*

or the *Kindertotenlieder*   some-
times new guests at the Hôtel des

Illusions ask the management to
throw her out but they are out-

voted by the others   she is the
songbird of their sadness   they

need her songs & want her to stay.

PARSIFAL: *Wagner's opera based on one of the Arthurian legends.*
WOZZECK: *opera based on a play by Buechner, by Alban Berg; one of
    the masterpieces of twentieth-century music.*
KINDERTOTENLIEDER: *song cycle by Gustav Mahler ("Songs on
    the Deaths of Children").*

THE OLD COMEDIAN

What part does that old man
think he is playing he is

rather funny but not very
his act is ridiculous and

even pathetic who does he
imagine he is surely he's

not the boy next door the
one the neighbors spoiled

and the teachers thought
was so promising but there

is a resemblance I'm afraid
it is the boy next door now

the old man is stumbling
and losing his lines he

must either be drunk or
sick will he die right on

the stage he's a comedian
and he wants the audience

to laugh at his funeral.

BOOK VI

EPIGRAMS

YOU'RE TROUBLE

aren't you asked the pretty
lady with whom I'd been con-

versing at the dinner party
I was trouble I told her when

I was young lots of trouble
but now I'm old and harmless.

THE OLD MAN'S LAMENT

He says that when the posthos
don't work no more it's like

the pain an amputee feels in
the foot that's been cut off.

THE GIFT

In that parking
lot pressure of

your body against
mine   iteration of

the dream of love

IN SCANDINAVIA

at country dances the
girls tuck the boys'

handkerchiefs in their
armpits and give them

back to be sniffed.

AT THE POST OFFICE

It makes his day when
by happy chance he en–

counters her on his morn-
ing visit to the post office

it's as if a rose had
opened to greet him.

HEART ISLAND

Stop searching stop weeping
she has gone to Heart Island

where the Truth People live
eating fern-shoots & berries

where there is no fighting
no sin no greed no sorrow

THE HAPPY POETS

What's happiness?
It's to lie side
By side in bed
Helping each other
Improve our poems.

THE TWO OF THEM

One kept his stomach full.
The other nourished his imagination.
It was a perfect arrangement
Until some confusion arose
As to which one should do which.

I SUPPOSE

the rhetoricians might call this
a variety of the pathetic fallacy

but when we talk on the telephone
I imagine I hear cunt in your voice

the soft slish of honey on silk as
Henry Miller used to describe it.

ELUSIVE TIME

In love it may be dangerous
to reckon on time to count

on it   time's here and then
it's gone   I'm not thinking

of death or disaster but of
the slippage the unpredictable

disappearance of days on which
we were depending for happiness.

SOME AMATORY EPIGRAMS
FROM THE GREEK ANTHOLOGY

Melissa pulled one reddish hair
From her braid and tied my hands
With it. I was her prisoner. I
Told her never to let me go.

Paulus Silentiarius (V, 230)

Sometimes secret love affairs
Yield more honey than those
Which are open.

Paulus Silentiarius (V, 219)

She kissed me one evening with
Wet lips; her mouth smelt sweet
As nectar. I'm drunk with her
Kiss. I have drunk love in
Abundance.

Anonymous (V, 305)

Melissa's beauty is the gift of
The god Eros; Aphrodite charmed
Her bed; the Graces gave her grace.

Meleager (V, 196)

In my heart Eros himself created
Sweet-voiced Melissa, the soul
Of my soul.

Meleager (V, 154)

Might it not be that someday in
Legend soft-gliding Melissa will
Surpass the Graces themselves?
                    Meleager (V, 148)

I swear, I swear it by Eros, I
Would rather hear her whisper in
My ear than listen to Apollo
Playing his lyre.
                    Meleager (V, 141)

I held her close, we were breast
To breast, hers supporting mine,
Her lips joined with mine. As for
The rest, the little bedlamp was the
Only witness; I am silent.
                    Marcus Argentarius (V, 128)

Her kiss is like the lime that
Catches birds. Her eyes are fire
And when she looks at me I also burn.
If she touches me she has me caught fast.
                    Meleager (V, 96)

I wish I were a rose, a pink rose,
For you to pick and press against
your snowy breasts.
                    Anonymous (V, 84)

Beauty without charm is only pleasing.
It's nothing to remember. It's like
Fishing with bait but no hook.
                    Capito (V, 67)

We fell in love, we kissed, you gave
Yourself to me, we had much pleasure.
But who am I, and who are you? How
did it happen that we came together?
Only the Kyprian goddess knows.

Anonymous (V, 51)

Gray are her lovely eyes, her cheeks
Of crystal. Could you not call her
Sweet mouth a rose? Her neck is of
Marble, her breasts smooth as marble.
Her small feet? They are more charming
Than those of silver-footed Thetis.

Rufinus (V, 48)

For so long, my darling, I prayed to
Have you with me at night, touching
And caressing. And now your love has
Brought me that happiness. You are
Beside me, naked. But why do I become
Drowsy? I owe you this felicity forever.

Rufinus (V, 47)

Beware a girl who is too ready.
But also one who hangs back too
Long. One is too quick, the other
Too slow. Look for one who is
Neither too plump nor too thin.
Too little flesh is as bad as too
Much. Never run to excesses.

Rufinus (V, 42 & 37)

Whether you have colored your hair
Dark or have it its natural shade,
It frames your dear face in beauty.
The god Eros loves your hair and
Will still be twining his fingers
In it when it is gray.

Anonymous (V, 26)

Shall we take a shower together,
Soaping ourselves and rubbing each
Other, flesh to flesh; then put on
Our robes and sip a good wine? The
season of such joys is short; then
Comes old age and finally death.

Rufinus (V, 12)

Make the bedlamp tipsy with oil;
It's the silent confidant of things
We seldom dare to speak of. Then
Let it go out. There are times when
The god Eros wants no living witness.
Close the door tight. Then let the
Bed, the lovers' friend, teach us
The rest of Aphrodite's secrets.

Philodemus (V, 4)

THE KYPRIAN: *Aphrodite was born on Cyprus.*
THETIS: *in Greek mythology one of the Nereids (sea nymphs),*
    the mother of Achilles.

BOOK VII

PENTASTICHS

A Note on the Form

A "pentastich" refers simply to a poem of five lines, without regard to metrics. The word is Greek derived, from *pentastichos,* though few examples survive from ancient times. In the *Greek Anthology,* there are some anonymous five-line epigrams, as well as one each by Empedocles, Palladas, Palladius, and (perhaps) the Emperor Constantine. Some other, later examples of five-line poems can be found in French, Italian, Spanish, and Chinese poetry. In English, the best-known five-liner is, of course, the limerick, though Tennyson and Poe used rhyming forms of five-line continuous stanzas. The most developed pentastich is the classic Japanese *tanka,* which influenced the American poet Adelaide Crapsey (1878–1914), whose unrhymed "cinquains" won her praise from Louis Untermeyer as an "unconscious imagist." Charles Olson's "fivers" in *The Maximus Poems* are in open form. The present selection of "Pentastichs" is of short-line compositions in natural voice cadence, many of them marginal jottings and paraphrases of commonplace book notations.

THE TENDER LETTER

C'était à Paris. She was Jeanine, young, pretty and
bright. Une jeune fille bien élevée. They often had
me to Sunday dinner. I thought we were just friends.
Then the note to my hotel: "Je voudrais être ta
maîtresse." In three months she was dead of cancer.

I TRAVEL YOUR BODY

I travel your body, like the world,
your belly is a plaza full of sun,
your breasts two churches where blood
performs its own, parallel rites,
my glances cover you like ivy . . .

"I travel your body. . . .": Octavio Paz, from Sunstone *(abridged),
translation by Eliot Weinberger.*

THE LIVING BRANCH

If I existed as a tree
I would not be a conifer, cone-bearing.
My nature would be deciduous, a long
Process of leaves, falling, falling
From the living branch.

Deborah Pease, the first stanza from a poem in The Feathered Wind.

ALL GOOD THINGS PASS

The girl at the order desk of the University
Press from whom I used to buy my Loeb Library
classics is now a telephone hitched to a
computer. She would wrap her long legs around
my neck and I imagined she was Tara of Cos.

THE SNAKE GAME

Henry looked like a shoeclerk but was a spell-
binder. He persuaded a friend to let him put a
garter snake into her vulva. Exciting at first
but then the snake wouldn't be pulled out. He
had to take her to the hospital emergency room.

Henry Miller.

THE LOCUST

Locust, beguiler of my loves and persuader of sleep,
mimic of nature's lyre, play for me a tune with your
talking wings to deliver me from the pains of care
and of love. In the morning I'll give you a fresh
green leek and drops of dew sprayed from my mouth.

Meleager of Gadara, fl. 60 B.C. (condensed).

THE IMMEASURABLE
BOUNDARIES

Heraclitus wrote that we would not discover
the boundaries of the soul even if we traveled
all the world's roads. At eighty I've traversed
a good many of them, but now I've stopped walking.
The boundaries of the soul are immeasurable.

THE HONEY BEE

You do everything, Melissa, just the
way your namesake the honey bee does.
When you're kissing me honey drips
from your lips, but when you ask
for money you have a sharp sting.

Marcus Argentarius (1st century A.D.).

PENELOPE TO ULYSSES

Penelope to the tardy Ulysses:
do not answer these lines, but come, for
Troy is dead and the daughters of Greece
rejoice. But all of Troy and Priam himself
are not worth the price I've paid for victory.

Ovid, from the Heroides, *translated by Howard Isbell.*

TANKA

In the *Dhammapada* it is written
that the body is a strong fortress
made up of bones, plastered with
flesh and blood, wherein lurk
pride, deceit, decay and death.

From the Dhammapada (1st century B.C.).

THE LONG FEET PEOPLE

Pliny relates in his *Natural History* that
in Iluria there's a race with feet a *pes*
long, turned backwards, with 16 toes. On
hot days they lie on their backs, using
their feet to shade themselves from the heat.

TWO FOR ONE

The painter Schiele knew he was two people,
and that he needed separate girls. When he
saw the Harms sisters in the street he hung
nude pictures of himself in his window. Edith
Harms married him. Adele became his model.

WORD SALAD

Neurologists call the babbling
of the patients in dementia "word
salad." Looking at recent verses
I realize that they are mostly
good examples of "word salad."

THE FANTASIST

Ronald Firbank the decadent novelist liked
to play out his fantasies. When Lady Cunard
invited him to lunch at the London Ritz he
studied the menu with care and ordered *one*
pea, which he sent back because it was cold.

THE PISSING OF THE TOADS

Concerning the venomous urine of toads, conceptions
are entertained which require consideration. That a
Toad pisseth, and this way diffuseth its venome,
is generally received, not only with us but also
in other parts, as the learned Scaliger observed.

From Thomas Browne's Pseudodoxia Epidemica, Enquiries into Certain
     Vulgar Errors *(1646)*.

THE WRITER AT WORK

On opening night of his play *Under Milk Wood,*
Dylan Thomas is backstage lying on his tummy
writing new lines for the cast: "Organ Morgan
at his bedroom window playing chords on the
sill for the fishwife gulls in Donkey Street."

THE GOD OF THE SUN AND FIRE

Glory to Agni, the high priest of the sacrifice.
We approach you, Agni, with reverential homage in
our thoughts, daily, both morning and evening.
You the radiant, the protector of sacrifices,
the constant illuminator, be as a father to us.

Excerpt from the First Mandala of the Rig Veda *(circa 1500 B.C.), abridged.*

THE MAGIC FLUTE

That summer in Munich we were Papageno and Papagena.
We walked along the Isar and in the Englische Garten
and went to a different opera almost every night. But
it was Mozart who set us dreaming and made us fall
in love. Beautiful days and now happy memories.

AN UNUSUAL GIRL

In Lucerne beautiful Birgita liked to circle
the Matterhorn in her Piper Cub. Evenings you
might find her with friends in her bathtub
enjoying live fish in an intimate way while
the phonograph played Schubert's *Trout Quintet*.

THE HETAERA

Ani Leasca, a Greek cocotte who worked Zurich,
could have modeled for Apelles. I never fingered
her expensive flesh, but when she wasn't engaged,
she liked to play pool in the Dolder, regaling
me with the kinks of the richest men in Europe.

THE RIGHT GIRL

Rufinus advised Thelon to beware a girl who seems
too eager. Or one who hangs back too long. One is
too quick, the other too slow. Look for one neither
too plump nor too thin. Too little flesh is as bad
as too much. Best, he said, never to run to excesses.

THE RESCUE

From New Orleans Tenn wrote me a wonderfully
comical letter. He was being relentlessly
pursued by a pretty girl. She was cramping
his style; would I get her off his back? A
very sexy girl; she soon had me on *my* back.

THE SCULPTOR

Brancusi didn't have much to say but he
cooked a great Romanian stew and liked
after eating to swing upside down by his
knees on a monkey's trapeze while his
phonograph blared out Ravel's *Bolero.*

GOOD PHILOSOPHY

When I give you an apple, if you love me
from your heart, exchange it for your
maidenhead. But if your feelings are what
I hope they are not, please take the apple
and reflect on how short-lived is beauty.

Plato (4th century B.C.).

AN EXQUISITE LIFE

Robert Montesquiou, the exquisite model
for Proust's Charlus, kept pet bats in
silver cages, and for his famous receptions
had each room of his dwelling sprayed
with a different suggestive perfume.

THE CRANE

Go away, crane! Leave the garden!
You have not told my love,
the prince of the seashore,
the torment that I suffer.
Go away, crane! Leave the garden!

Lines from the Tamil of the Shilappadikaram *(3rd century A.D.), translated
by Alain Daniélou.*

THE INVITATION TO MAKE LOVE

Show her drawings of animals making love, then
of humans. The sight of erotic creatures such
as geese will make her curious. Write amorous
messages to her on palm leaves. Tell her your
dreams about her. Tickle her toes with your finger.

Excerpts from the Sanskrit of Vatsyayana's Kama Sutra *(circa 5th century
A.D.), translated by Alain Daniélou.*

BOOK VIII

PERMANET MEMORIA

Age has done its dreaded work.
We are no longer what we were
When we met by the Aegean shore
And discovered we loved one another.
Now our hair is white and our limbs
Are weak, our skin is wrinkled,
There is no desire to be satisfied.
But there is still memory.
Let us give thanks to the kind god
Who provides the consolation of memory.
We can enflesh ourselves in memory.

PERMANET MEMORIA: *the survival of memory.*

EASTER IN PITTSBURGH

Even on Easter Sunday
when the church was a

jungle of lilies and
ferns fat Uncle Paul

who loved his liquor
so would pound away

with both fists on the
stone pulpit shouting

sin sin sin and the
fiery fires of hell

and I cried all after-
noon the first time I

heard what they did to
Jesus it was something

the children shouldn't
know about till they

were older but the new
maid told me and both

of us cried a lot and so
mother got another one

right away and she sent
away Miss Richardson

who came all the way
from England because

she kept telling how
her fiancé Mr. Bowles-

Lyon died suddenly of
a heart attack he just

said one day at lunch
I'm afraid I'm not well

and the next thing they
knew he was sliding un-

der the table. Easter
was nice the eggs were

silly but the big lilies
were wonderful & when

Uncle Paul got so fat
from drinking that he

couldn't squeeze into
the pulpit anymore he

had to preach from the
floor there was an el-

ders' meeting and they
said they would have

the pulpit rebuilt but
Uncle Paul said no it

was the Lord's manifest
will and he would pass

his remaining years in
sacred studies. I liked

Thanksgiving better be-
cause that was the day

father took us down to
the mills but Easter I

liked next best and the
rabbits died because we

fed them beet tops and
the lamb pulled up the

grass by the roots and
was sold to Mr. Page the

butcher. I asked Uncle
Robert what were sacred

studies he said he was
not really sure but he

guessed they came in a
bottle and mother sent

me away from the table
when I wouldn't eat my

lamb chops that was
ridiculous she said it

wasn't the lamb of God
it was just Caesar An–

dromache Nibbles but I
couldn't I just wouldn't

and the year of the strike
we didn't go to church

at all on Easter because
they said it wasn't safe

down town so instead we
had prayers in the library

and then right in the mid–
dle the telephone rang it

was Mr. Shupstead at the
mill they had to use

tear gas father made a
special prayer right a–

way for God's protection
& mercy and then he sent

us out to the farm with
mother we stayed a week

and missed school but it
rained a lot and I broke

the bathroom mirror and
had to learn a long psalm.

WHAT THE PENCIL WRITES

Often when I go out I
put in my coat pocket

some paper and a pen-
cil in case I want to

write something down
well there they are

wherever I go and as
my coat moves the pen-

cil writes by itself
a kind of gibberish

hieroglyphic which I
often think as I un-

dress at night and take
out those papers with

nothing written on
them but strange &

meaningless marks is
the story of my life.

DIE BEGEGNUNG

It was in a dark forest
Where one night I was lost
Donner und Blitz
   Erfüllung und Verlust
      Schmerzen und Wonne
         Gelächter und Tränen
I encountered a hooded figure
Who was my other self
He gave me his hand and fair words
And followed me back to this city
Where he has never left my side
   Sorge und Freude
      Einsicht und Zweifel
My other self, my constant companion.

A PARABLE

Once upon a time when I
was about eight Papa took

me with him to lunch at
the house of Mrs R   she

was very beautiful and
gave me two helpings

of ice cream   after lunch
Papa told me to go out in-

to the yard to play   I
climbed a tree and look-

ed in a window   Papa and
Mrs R were doing strange

things   they were lying on
the bed and had no clothes

on   this was a long time
ago but I still see them

there doing strange things.

THE STORY OF RHODOPE

has always attracted me   she
was the Thracian courtesan

who lost her slipper while
bathing   but an eagle picked

it up and dropped it in the
lap of Pharaoh Psammetichus

who of course searched her
out and married her loading

her with gold bracelets   the
story is important to me be-

cause my father had a shoe
fetish   he would take one

of his dollbabies into Del-
man's on Fifth Avenue and

buy her a dozen pairs of
slippers at a crack   dear

old dad I'm happy that their
pretty footsies made you glad

you weren't a book reader and
you needed some literary love.

AVE ATQUE VALE

(my father)

I sat on the edge of the bed
and held his hand   it was dry

and cold   I squeezed the hand
but of course there was no re-

sponse   they had dressed him
in one of his Scottish tweed

suits with the deer's-horn
buttons on the side pockets

and put on the Princeton
(orange and black) tie   I

had come to say goodbye   I
was crying but suddenly my

sadness changed to resent-
ment even to anger almost

to hatred   why are you de-
serting me   how dare you

leave me   in my rage I
pulled up his shoulders

and shook him as hard as
I could   I raised him

further and banged his head
against the pillow   I want-

ed to make him open his eyes
how can you abandon me   you

the one who loved me most.

THE WILD ANEMONE

(for Ann)

I'll call it the daring
flower its softness its

pallor so little suggesting
the strength with which

it fights the wind its
petals so delicate it

seems a touch would wither
them yet they'll outlast a

three-day storm and will
outlast I think [and now

I speak to her] the tempests
that a foolish heart invents

to plague itself because
it hardly dares to love

the wild anemone
the daring flower.

THE EMPTY ROOM

(my wife Ann)

As he passes the open door
he can see there is no long-

er anyone in the room   no one
is lying in the bed and no

one is attending the recum-
bent figure   the water glass

with its bent drinking straw
is gone from the bedside ta-

ble   there are no flowers
in the vase none of her fa-

vorite red and blue anemo-
nes   the window shades have

been raised because the
room need no longer be

kept darkened   now sun-
light is flooding the

room   in its neatness
and emptiness it is for

him a scene of terror
what can he do with

what is left of his life?

THE APSARASES

I think someone is watching
Me. Someone is following me,
I'm sure, but is not visible.
How do I know I'm being
Followed? There are little
Sounds of someone walking
Behind me, sounds as soft
As the flutter of a bird's
Wings, but when I turn around
There is no one there. And
Sometimes if I wake up in
The night I sense there is
Someone in the darkness. One
Day I walked on the beach
And there were strange marks
On the sand but they weren't
Like footprints. I suppose
I should be frightened but
I'm not.

In the puranas of Hindu
Mythology we may read of
The apsarases, sacred nymphs,
Who can make themselves
Invisible, and who can fly
Great distances, even over
The oceans. One of their
Roles is to protect and
Guide persons whom the gods
Have chosen to find dhamma-
Pada, the true way, the
Path to virtue and wisdom.

THE JUNK COLLECTOR

What bothers me most about
the idea of having to die

(sooner or later) is that
the collection of junk I

have made in my head will
presumably be dispersed

not that there isn't more
and better junk in other

heads & always will be but
I have become so fond of

my own head's collection.

MY OLD GRAY SWEATER

in the back of the closet   what
will you do with it the one with

buttons down the front the heavy
one I used to wear when I could

still cut firewood what will you
do with it the Salvation Army I

guess some worthy & needy man
can still get a lot of use out

of it but you know I'd really
rather not please take it out

into the woods and nail it to
that big oak Gary jokes that

he wants to re-enter the food
chain he wants to be eaten by

a bear I'd like my sweater just
to rot away in the woodlands let

the birds peck at it and build
their nests with the gray wool

please nail me to the big oak.

GARY: *the poet and environmentalist Gary Snyder.*

IS MEMORY

Something we have
Or something we've lost?
How much remains of what
Happened when it first took place?
I imagine that I see you clearly,
Every detail of our first embrace,
That I still hear each word you spoke,
And the tones of your voice
As you spoke them. Yet how much
Of what comes back may be illusion,
Born of longing for what
Might later have been?

THE HOUSE OF LIGHT

has been designed by the master
builder but the workmen have not

been able to build it the car-
penters & the masons have toil-

ed for many years but they can-
not find a way to make their ma-

terials adhere to enclose light
every method has been a failure

neither lumber nor stone not even
metal or glass will serve to hold

in the light it always escapes
and returns to its source can

anyone build the house of light?

THOSE TO COME

Will those who come after us
remember who we were except for
three or four generations of
family? Will there be a child
who amuses herself by going
through cartons of old letters
in the attic? Will she draw
crayon pictures of the people
she reads about, showing what
she imagines we were like?

I'd be a fool to hope that any
of my verses would remain in
print. I must value them by
the amusement I have in composing
them. Just that, nothing more.

But what happened to make me
grow old so soon? When I was
young I never thought of old
age, of what it would be like.
And why can I recall only part
of some scene I'd like to relive
now? Where have the lost fragments
gone? As I lie wakeful in bed
what I see is a long corridor
of closed doors.

SWAPPING MINDS

(for Vanessa)

Melissa and I were sitting
by the little lake in Green
Park in London playing
"swapping minds." It's an
old game that came down from
the Lowlands. It was a fine
day so we had brought
a little picnic. Melissa
makes wonderful pâté, as
good as anything from Fortnum
& Masson. Yummy. And we had
a half bottle of Chardonnay
between us.

Here is how the game of
"swapping minds" goes. It's
not a child's game, it's
very intellectual, or should
I say psychological. Just
imagine Melissa and I are
talking. She says something
to me, "James why are you
always so arrogant?" But,
obviously that's not what
she is thinking. To answer
her I must try to imagine
what she *was* thinking when
she asked that. I must swap
minds with her.
I ventured the following:
"Melissa, you have the most

lovely white skin in England,
you must be careful not to
get sunburned.

Melissa: "James, why do you
pretend you are Scots when
you're really of Irish descent?"

James: "Melissa, are you
remembering the handsome
Russian boy you met in the
Hermitage on your trip to
Russia and he took you to have
an ice cream with him?"

Melissa: "James, did the
other boys in school tease
you because you were so bad
at games?"

James: "Do you really love
me or are you just flirting?"

Melissa: "I'm sorry, James,
but the response is in your
mind, not in mine."

That was the end of the
"swapping game" for that
day, and such a happy day
it was, there in Green Park,
watching the ducks on the
pond.

STEP ON HIS HEAD

Let's step on daddy's head shout
the children my dear children as
we walk in the country on a sunny

summer day my shadow bobs dark on
the road as we walk and they jump
on its head and my love of them

fills me all full of soft feelings
now I duck with my head so they'll
miss when they jump they screech

with delight and I moan oh you're
hurting you're hurting me stop and
they jump all the harder and love

fills the whole road but I see it run
on through the years and I know
how some day they must jump when

it won't be this shadow but really
my head (as I stepped on my own
father's head) it will hurt really

hurt and I wonder if then I will
have love enough will I have love
enough when it's not just a game?

THE CALVES

On the road to Canaan there is
a big dairy farm   beside the

barn there are rows of little
houses like white boxes   calves

are chained to them   they are
fed only milk and not allowed

to wander or they wouldn't be
tender veal   my soft-hearted

granddaughter asks me to stop
the car   she wants to go down

to pet them and comfort them
I say the farmer might not like

that it would be trespassing
I tell her that there are also

people who are chained to boxes
but she doesn't understand me

the whole of life lies before her.

EXPERIENCE OF BLOOD

I never knew there was so much blood
in a man until my son killed himself

he did it with a kitchen knife stab-
bing himself all over and cutting his

wrists   then he got into the bathtub
and died there in the water   that's

where we found him   but could he have
changed his mind for a moment   the floor

was a carpet of blood & blood was spat-
tered on the walls the basin was cov-

ered with blood   did he stand there
looking at himself in the mirror still

wondering who he really was and then
went on with it   I had to wipe away the

blood   it took me four hours to do it
but I couldn't have asked anyone else

because after all it was my blood too.

IN OLD AGE

The pace of time changes
And is strangely bifurcated.
Day to day it races along,
Too fast for enjoyment.
The sled is careening down the hill
Toward the big oak where it will crash.
But at night, as I lie sleepless,
Time seems hardly to move.
Each scene that passes through my head
Is almost stationary,
Often lingering longer than I can bear.

AN ELEGY OF MIMNERMUS

How much joy is left in life
Without the blessing of foam-
Born Aphrodite? Let me die now
That I can no longer have love
Secrets and the gifts of desire
And the pleasures of soft beds.
These were the blossomings of
Youth, giving happiness both
To young men and their lovers.
But age brings aches and bad
Smells to the man who has
Grown old. It makes evil
Flourish in his body and
Mind. It wears down the heart.
For him the warmth of sunlight
Is diminished. Children fear
Him and women despise him.
Cruel is the treatment with
Which the gods punish old age.

An imitation.

LOST

Some of my friends have all
The luck when it comes to
Dreams. They have such a variety
Of wonderful, exciting dreams:
Dreams about sexy mysterious
Girls; dreams about stupendous
Meals in Parisian restaurants:
Mystical dreams that can be
Interpreted in interesting ways.
I have only one dream that is
Always the same. I'm lost in
A huge foreign city where I've
Never been. I'm afraid I'm
Going to miss an important
Appointment if I can't find
My way. Someone very important
But I can't remember his name.
There are people in the streets
But they don't speak English.
I get frightened. I begin to
Run from street to street. I
Run faster and faster till I
Wake up. Where is that city?

IMPRISONED

(for Gertrude)

It has been a long sentence for you
In the prison of my gloom
Where I sit scribbling verses
In my untidy room.

I could read to you from old books,
But what would that avail?
You're of the merry world,
I of my lonely cell.

Do you ever suspect how much I love you,
For that is what is true,
As I scribble my quare rhymes,
Rhymes that I make for you.

QUARE: *Irish dialect, queer.*

DO THEY MAKE LOVE?

Don't pick at it, my nurse says,
It won't get well if you pick at it.

I've never seen him but I think
I know what he looks like.

I know it itches but if you don't
Leave it alone it will get worse.

I can't guess what he says to her
But I hear what his voice sounds like.

Remember what happened to Albert,
His leg got infected from scratching.

I don't dare imagine that he touches
Her, or that she touches him.

Albert had to go to the hospital,
They nearly had to amputate his leg.

If he touches her I want him to die.

OUR BICYCLES

"At Versailles only the Queen may have pompons on her coach-covers; fastened with nails, and of any colour that she pleases. Duchesses have blue covers. Wives of eldest sons of dukes have red covers. Widows have black velvet."
—THE DUC DE SAINT-SIMON
Historical Memoirs

My brother being the eldest had
for his bike the most elaborate

accoutrements   a pair of squirrel
tails (one grey one brown) which

flew from his handlebars   Cousin
Ham had an extra gear for attack-

ing the hills of Shadyside where
we lived   Cousin Georgie (the shy

one) had two bells with different
tones but when he took his hands

off the bars trying to sound both
of them at once his front wheel

swerved and he ended up at the
hospital for 4 stitches   as for

me (the youngest) I was still on
a tricycle and had nothing but

tears when the others sped on a-
head of me (wait for me wait for

me I would cry) leaving me far be-
hind wailing and eating their dust.

HIC JACET

civis pulvis et nihil
was all the inscription

that Cardinal Portecarrero
permitted on his tomb in

the cathedral at Toledo   he
would not even allow his

name to be inscribed on it
just a flat stone with no

barrier around it so that
everyone would walk on him

a realistic man and though
he didn't know it a good

Buddhist   here lie ashes
dust and nothingness R I P.

MOMENTS IN SPACE

No exact moment is recorded for
When I left time and entered
Space; nothing precise that I
Could put down in my diary. The
Journalists were vague about it,
Using condolent euphemisms that
Weren't believed (there had been
So many cries of "wolf"). The lady
Judge at the probate court was
Annoyed. "I *must* have a date,"
She said. It was gradual, not
What I'd anticipated. It reminded
Me of dirty water running out
Of a bathtub with a little swirl
And sucking sound when it was
All empty. Of course everyone
In the village knew something
Was happening. I would meet them
In the pharmacy or at the post
Office and not remember the
Names of people I'd known for
Fifty years. I think they'll
Miss me; I gave them a lot of
Laughs, the village eccentric.

It's too soon to give much of
A report on space. I'm just
Beginning to get my bearings.
No asteroids or astronauts in
Their capsules so far. No trees
Or grass but beautiful cloud
Formations. It's a relief not
To have to bother with eating.

Few people around and none
I'd met in books. (I'd like
To see Godot again.) But space
Is endless, it stretches out
To nowhere. I may be a million
Light years away in space.

DE CONTEMPTU MORTIS

What is consciousness that it
Leaves us when most we need it
To save what little we have
Managed to construct? Will the
Pale torch of loving soon be
Sputtering out for me? The
Children joke at table whether
Grandfather should be buried
Or burned. What difference
Could it make? Does their humor
Mask any affection that will
Last when life takes them by
Their little necks and shakes
Them as it can, rich or poor?
Tell me a happy fable that
Off in a distant galaxy some
Creature with three eyes is
Watching over me? That can't
Be so, believe me, it's not so;
Walk up or down, turn right
Or left, it isn't so. We came,
We breathed a bit of air, we go.

DE CONTEMPTU MORTIS: *in contempt of death.*

THE DEPARTURE

They say I have to go away soon
On the long trip to nowhere.
Put things in order, they say.
But I've always been disorderly
So why start that now?
Not much time, they say.
What to do with it?
Not much different, I think,
Than what I've been doing.
My best friends have always been
The ones in books.
Read a few pages here, a few there.
No complaints, few regrets,
Thanks to everybody.

BOOK IX

from BYWAYS

Segments from a Long-Poem-in-Progress

A Note on the Metric

In composing the long autobiographical poem "Byways," a work-in-progress of which the pages that follow are segments, I am intentionally avoiding rhetoric and verbal decoration. I would like to achieve a tone of colloquial speech and a pace for fast reading. Let's call "Byways" narrative verse. It is certainly not lyrical poetry. A friend has called it a suitable receptacle for recollections. I owe the metric to my old friend and mentor Kenneth Rexroth. He perfected the essentially three-beat line in his travel poem *The Dragon & The Unicorn,* which I published at New Directions in 1941.

An Honest Heart . . . A Knowing Head

Thomas Jefferson counsels a student. Excerpts from a letter to Peter Carr, written in 1785.

. . . Time now begins to be precious
to you. Every day you lose, will
retard a day your entrance on that
public stage whereon you may begin
to be useful to yourself. However,
the way to repair the loss is to
improve the future time. I trust,
that with your dispositions, even
the acquisition of science is a
pleasing employment. I can assure
you, that the possession of it is,
what (next to an honest heart)
will above all things render you
dear to your friends, and give
you fame and promotion . . .
Give up money, give up fame,
give up science, give the
earth itself and all it contains,
rather than do an immoral act.
And never suppose that in any
possible situation, or under
any circumstances, it is best
for you to do a dishonorable
thing, however slightly so it
may appear to you. . . .

From the practice of the purest
virtue, you may be assured you
will derive the most sublime
comforts in every moment of

life, and in the moment of death. . . .
An honest heart being the first
blessing, a knowing head is the
second. It is time for you now
to be choice in your reading;
to begin to pursue a regular
course in it; and not to suffer
yourself to be turned to the
right or left by reading any
thing out of that course. . . .

For the present, I advise you
to begin a course of antient
history, reading everything in
the original and not in translations.
First read Goldsmith's history
of Greece. This will give you a
digested view of that field.
Then take up antient history
in the detail, reading the
following books in the
following order: Herodotus,
Thucydides, Xenophontis
Hellenica, Anabasis,
Arrian, Quintus Curtius,
Diodorus Siculus, Justin.

This shall form the first
stage of your historical
reading, and is all I should
mention to you now. The
next, will be of Roman
history; Livy, Sallust,
Caesar, Cicero's epistles,
Suetonius, Tacitus, Gibbon.

From that we will come down
to modern history.

In Greek and Latin poetry,
you have read or will read
at school: Virgil, Terence,
Horace, Anacreon, Theocritus,
Homer, Euripides, Sophocles.
Read also Milton's Paradise
Lost, Shakespeare, Ossian,
Pope's and Swift's works, in
order to form your style in
your own language. In
morality, read Epictetus,
Xenophontis Memorabilia,
Plato's Socratic dialogues,
Cicero's philosophies,
Antoninus, and Seneca. . . .

Give about two hours of
every day to exercise;
for health must not be
sacrificed to learning. A
strong body makes the mind
strong. As to the species
of excercise, I advise the
gun. While this gives a
moderate exercise to the
body, it gives boldness,
enterprise, and independence
to the mind. Games played
with the ball, and others
of that nature, are too
violent for the body, and
stamp no character on the
mind. Let your gun

therefore be the constant
companion of your walks.
Never think of taking a
book with you. The object
of walking is to relax the mind.
You should therefore not permit
yourself even to think while you
walk; but divert your attention
by the objects surrounding you.
Walking is the best possible
excercise. Habituate yourself
to walk very far. The Europeans
value themselves on having
subdued the horse to the uses
of man; but I doubt whether
we have not lost more than we
have gained, by the use of
this animal. No one has
occasioned so much, the
degeneracy of the human
body. An Indian goes on
foot nearly as far in a
day, for a long journey,
as an enfeebled white does
on his horse; and he will
tire the best horses. . . .

You are now, I expect
learning French. You must
push this; because the
books which will be put
into your hands when you
advance into Mathematics,
Natural philosophy, Natural
history, etc will be mostly

French, these sciences being
better treated by the French
than the English writers.
Our future connection
with Spain renders that
the most necessary of
the modern languages,
after the French. When
you become a public man,
you may have occasion
for it, and the circumstance
of your possessing that
language, may give you a
preference over other
candidates. I have
nothing further to
add for the present, but
husband well your time,
cherish your instructors,
strive to make everybody
your friend, and be
assured, that nothing
will be so pleasing
as your success, to,
dear Peter.
Your's affectionately,
Thomas Jefferson.

The Wrong Bed—Moira

It was in London that I
Fell into the wrong bed.
I should have guessed she
Was paranoid but sometimes
You can't tell. She picked
Me up in the Gargoyle. It
Was the night Dylan tripped
And sprained his ankle so
Badly he couldn't walk. We
Got him to his place in a
Taxi, then went on to hers
In Chelsea. I think her
Name was Moira but I can't
Remember for sure now. She
Was a small girl, brown hair,
Lively eyes, nicely dressed,
An upper-class accent, quite
Chatty. She had some bottles
And we drank till we both
Passed out with our clothes
On. Next day, about noon,
She ordered a car with a
Driver and we drove down to
Bath. That's when the bad talk
About Americans started, but
I let it pass. She had friends
In Bath, a couple with an
Apartment in the Crescent.
We dumped on them; they said
We could have the sofa. We
Ate at a pub, then the drink
Began again. I think I was
The first to pass out. I woke

Up in the night. She was on
The sofa with the man. No sign
Of the wife, I went back
To sleep on the floor.

Next morning when the couple
Had gone off, they had a
Shop somewhere, she said,
"Well, you brought me down
Here, I guess I'd better
Let you have it." She sat
Down on the sofa and pulled
Up her skirt. By then I
Wasn't interested, but she
Jibed at me: "Come on, Yank,
Let's see what you're good
For." When that was over,
And it wasn't much, there
Was the only kind word I
Heard about Americans. She
Said, "You're better than
Most of the Johnnies around
Here." I should have left
Her in Bath to get herself
Home, but I felt sorry for
Her somehow. She was a mess
But sort of pitiful. I got
Her back to Chelsea. She
Didn't ask me in. The car
Hires ran me sixty pounds.

The Desert in Bloom

Why can't you remember the Nevada
Desert awash with bright-colored
Flowers when we camped not far
From Tonopah that April long ago?
It was soon after we had met in
San Francisco and fallen in love.
You were George's sister, the
Beautiful poet's beautiful sister,
That's how I got to know you.
Surely you must remember how the
Desert that was so harsh all the
Rest of the year, rocks and gray
Sand, had suddenly burst into
Bloom, a salute to Persephone in
Almost violent praise of spring,
A salute that would last only a
Few weeks till the snow moisture
In the ground would be exhausted.
Rexroth had loaned us a tent and
We gathered dry cactus to cook
Over an open fire. At night we
Heard the soft cooing of doves
From all around us in the dark
But at dawn they ceased their
Complaining. You said that they
Reminded you of the doves in
Provence when you were there
As a girl, the *roucoulement des
Colombes* that the troubadours
And their ladies had heard in
The castle gardens, recording
Their sound in their *cansos.*

The ground was hard under our
Sleeping bags, the desert gets
Chilly at night, so cold that
Sometimes we had to squeeze
Into one bag, skin to skin,
Enlaced together. At night in the
Desert the stars seem twice as
Bright as anywhere else; when
We lay on our backs we would
Look up into the vastness, trying
To locate the constellations
And remember the names that were
Given them by the Greeks in the
Myths how many thousands of years
Ago. Andromeda and the Dioscuri,
Cassiopeia, whom Perseus saved
From the sea-monster; Orion, the
Mighty hunter; the Pleiades, whose
Comings and goings tell the seasons;
Berenike, whose pretty lock of
Hair has lived in song; the lion,
The dragon, and the swan. Your
People were Jewish but your
Beauty was more of Attica than
Of Phoenicia, great brown eyes,
Dark hair and olive skin. The
Girls of Lesbos would have adored
You but you were not of their
Kind. Your body is described
In the *Song of Songs;* not a
Fraction of an inch would
Have changed in its proportions
If I were a sculptor. The desert
Was empty and I would ask you
To lie naked in the sun, now
And then changing your pose, a

Moving sculpture. You had the
Marks of Eros, a girl fit for
The Mysteries. Liquid as the
Fountain Arethusa. And you were
Funny and endearing and passionate.
Holding hands, we took walks on
The endless desert before the sun
Became too hot. I picked flowers
And made a multicolored garland
For your hair. The handmaiden
Of Aphrodite, *venerandam*. In the
Shade of the tent I read you the
Exquisite love sonnets of Louise
Labé, which aroused me to make
Love again, hot as it was, the
Sweat glistening on our bodies.

One day we drove into Tonopah,
Now the slumbering ruin of the
Old hell-&-damnation mining
Town, where once fortunes of
Gold were won and lost at the
Tables, and men killed for it.
The streets were empty, but in
What is left of the Grand Hotel
California we found an old man
Dozing on top of the green
Gaming table; we woke him up
And shot craps with silver dollars
For chips. We stayed on the desert
For three days, when we had used
Up the water we had brought in
Cans.

Now after fifty years we're in
Touch again. You've had four

Husbands and I'm on my third
Marriage. You say that you
Can hardly remember our love-
Making on the flowering desert.
How can that be? For me it's
As fresh as if it only happened
Yesterday. I see you clear with
My garland in your hair. Now we
Are two old people nursing our
Aches. What harm can there be
In remembering? We cannot hurt
One another now.

In Trivandrum

My next step in India that year
(Which was 1953, as best I can
Recall) was Trivandrum, a little
But lovely city in the region now
Known as Kerala, which was in
Colonial times a princely state
Ruled by the Portuguese, then
The Dutch, and then the English,
Who called it Cochin. Vasco da
Gama landed his ships at
Cochin in 1502, reckoning it the
Finest port on the Arabian Sea
South of Bombay. Cochin has a
Heavy rainfall, making the land
Rich for rice, tapioca, pepper and
Vegetables. The landscape is set
With graceful coconut palms and
Many ponds and little ornamental
Waterways. The language mainly
Is Malayalam, but Trivandrum
Holds also a settlement of Jews
That boasts the oldest synagogue
In Asia. Christians of differing
Sects are scattered all over the
Subcontinent. Many myths tell
Of the coming of Christianity
To India. In Malabar they think
The Apostle Thomas ("doubting
Thomas") arrived in Cochin in
A.D. 52 to take up the work of
Conversion. But on the eastern
Coast people tell you Thomas
Built his church in Madras on
A hill known as The Mount.

I had come to Trivandrum to
Meet the novelist Raja Rao.
Along with R. K. Narayan of
Mysore, Raja Rao was, in those
Days and probably still is, the best
Indian writer working in English.
(How good the native writers
May be, since they compose in
thirteen major languages, is
Hard to guess. Few of them can
Read the works of the others.)
But I had read Raja Rao's novel
The Serpent and the Rope and I
Had no doubt in my mind that
He was first class. I had heard
Rumors that he had finished
A new novel. I wanted to find
Him. The rumors were true.
After we had been together for
Two days, during which Raja
Had assessed my enthusiasm
For Indian life and culture, he
Placed the manuscript of his
New book, *Kanthapura,* in my
Hands, saying: "I think you'll
Like this. My friend Mr. Forster
Has been over it and says it's
A good book about India as
She is today, after Gandhi."
I didn't need Forster's praise to
Convince me that this was a
Masterpiece. *Kanthapura* is
A book like no other I'd read,
A magical book that brings the
Spell of India to the western
Reader. New Directions brought

The book out at once, and after
Many reprintings it remains
As fresh and compelling as it
Was when I first encountered it.

"Kanthapura" is a typical small
Village of southern India in
Which the changing life of all
Castes, impacted by Gandhi's
Revolution of independence
From the British, is the main
Force. Young Moorthy back
From the city with "new ideas,"
Works to break down the old
Barriers. Nonviolence, as
Gandhi taught it, is his way
Of mobilizing the villagers to
Action. But his efforts are met
With violence from the police
And the rich landowners. The
Remarkable thing in the book
To me is its colloquial manner.
Rao's narrator is an old woman
Of the village who is imbued
With the legendary history of
Her region, the old traditions
Of Hinduism and the Vedic
Myths. She knows the past.
The stories of the villagers,
And her commentary on her
Neighbors is both pungent and
Wise. In her speech are echoes
Of the traditional folk-epics
Such as the *Ramayana*. But
How does Rao manage this
When writing in plain lucid

English? He has somehow
Made us hear native speech
In his narrator's extraordinary
Anglo-Indian language. He
Has a fine ear. He had known
The intonations and rhythms
Of the villagers as a child when
He was growing up in Mysore.
Then, because he came from
A prominent family, he had
Opportunities unusual for
An Indian, the University of
Madras and study in France at
Montpellier and the Sorbonne.

Traipsing about the countryside
With Raja as my guide was a
Great pleasure. The land is so
Verdant, and the busy life of
The inland waterways delighted
Me, the small open ferryboats,
Mostly motorized but now and
Then a boat with the red lateen
Sails of the ancient Arab dhows
That had first opened up the
Malabar coast. Raja had no
Car, but we borrowed bicycles
With which we followed the
Footpaths or the rough roads
Created by old bullock carts
Whose once-round wheels
Had been worn squarish by
Long use. We saw the villagers
Ploughing with their cattle,
Humped slaves who would work
Every day until they dropped,
Sleeping nights out in the rain.

Yet these cows seemed to live
A happier life than the sacred
Cows you find in Calcutta who
Live in the streets, sleep on the
Sidewalks and are fed by the
Faithful—once I was watching
As children gave candy bars
To a Calcutta cow—all this
Because the people believe
That cattle are descended, at
Least symbolically, from those
The Gopis watched over for
Lord Krishna at Brindaban.
We saw sheep and chickens
Around the hutments but no
Pigs. Little monkeys aplenty in
The coconut palms. The men
Distill a palm wine which they
Call "toddy." We were offered
Cups of it which tasted so awful
I could scarcely get mine down
Out of politeness. It looked like
Rotten eggs. But the intoxicating
Effect is said to be considerable.
Knowing Malayalam, Raja Rao
Was able to converse with the
People, who were not shy. They
Gathered around us to talk and
Raja interpreted for me. He said
They had never seen anyone
As tall as I (I'm six foot five).
They wanted to know where I
Came from and what I ate to
Get so big. Did I practice yoga?
Or some other occult mastery?

Some of them invited us into
Their thatched huts to show
Us with pride the rice-paste
Abstract paintings on their
Walls and thresholds. Raja
Taught me on that visit to
Eat curry and other Indian
Foods with my fingers, for no
Brahmin would ask for utensils.
It would be a breach of the rules
Of caste. But don't ask me to
Show you how it's done; I was
A poor pupil. The weather was
Hot in Cochin, of course, all
That moisture with the sun
Smoldering down through it.
Raja loaned me a dhoti, much
Better than my European pants
And shirt. But I managed more
Than once to get the skirt of
My dhoti caught in my bicycle
Chain, with resultant tumbles.
Our audience was amused. In
The evenings we had our curry
At Raja's home, which was for
Me a further trial of the fingers
In place of a fork. His was an
Extended family living in a
Small house in Trivandrum
And to this day I'm not sure
Who was who. Many women
In their saris smiled at me and
Said nothing. Only the men
Joined us at table. The women
Ate apart, maybe in the kitchen

Which I was not shown. Then
Raja and I went out to wander
The streets of the old town with
Its Dutch-style buildings. Parts
Of it could have been Delft or
Nijmegen. No street lights, not
Much light from the house
Windows; it was eerie. Bare
Feet in the darkness making
No noise. It was enchanting too.

We went to a show by
A troupe of Kathakali dancers
—Very exciting. Most of the
Dancing in South India, such
As the gliding style of Bharata
Natya, is tranquil, except for
An accompaniment of soft
Drumming; movement is
By the arms and hands, and
The "story" is told in classic
Mudras that have assigned
Meanings. Kathakali however
Is the opposite, violent motion
Most of the time. In a way it
Reminded me of the dramatic
Posturing in Japanese Kabuki.
For the westerner one of the
Attractions of Kathakali is
The costumes. Also the masks
Of the male dancers, sculpted
And grotesque. Vivid primary
Colors. Faces to scare children.
Demons and heroes. Men as
Tigers, as serpents. Terrifying.
Much magic, much death.

The plays are given outdoors
And always at night, often not
Finishing until the dawn. In
Darkness the great brass lamps
Flicker and add to the mystery.
The audience sits on the ground
(Though Raja Rao and I were
Honored with chairs). Men,
Women and children usually
Are separated. Two drummers,
Sounding their drums with
Their hands, often in very fast
Rhythms, provide the music.
The actors speak passages of
Verse that narrate the action
Of the play. The dialogue is
Sung by two singers who stand
At the back of the "stage." Now
The stories of the plays are told
In Malayalam rather than the
Classic Sanskrit, but they are
Still the ancient texts, epics like
The *Ramayana* (which reports
The heroic adventures of Rama
When he rescues his wife from
The demon-king Ravana of
Ceylon) or the *Mahabharata*
(Which recounts the endless
Struggle between two families,
The Pandavas and Kauravas,
Though the pre-eminent hero
Of the poem is the god Krishna)
Or the *Gita Govinda* (a cycle of
Poems about Krishna). These
Are traditional tales known
Almost universally in India

To all classes, just as Greek
Myths and Bible stories
Are known to us in the West.
In origin they go back perhaps
A dozen thousand years to
The oral tradition of village
Storytellers, the entertainers
Of that culture, just as our
Homeric epics are thought
To have been composed and
Revised and embellished by
Generations of warrior poets
Who recited them around the
Smoky campfires of ancient
Armies. At some point these
Original Hindu poems were
Transcribed into Sanskrit by
The pandits and gurus. Then
The final step was translation
Into the various vernaculars,
Hindi, Urdu, Tamil, Marathi,
Malayalam, and many others.
The evening of Kathakali was
Dramatic and thrilling though
Very long: it went on way past
Midnight. Raja Rao briefed me
On the unfolding motifs and
Actions as the play progressed.
Then the next day at dusk we
Experienced something even
More remarkable. Through Rao
I had met Professor Vivekananda
Who taught in the college at
Ernakulam on the coast north
Of Trivandrum. Vivekananda
Knew Sri Nalanda, a Vedantist

Guru from Bombay who was
Visiting friends in a small
Village in the Cardamon
Hills. It was a rough trip
Getting there in a jitney
But we made it and the sage
Welcomed us cordially to one
Of the most intense occasions
Of my visit. I wouldn't have
Believed the background story
Vivekananda told me about Sri
Nalanda if we had been in any
Country but India, where the
Occurrence of wonders is so
Continual and many minds
Are saturated with the occult.
Gurus, holy men, sadhus, yogis.
Sannyasis all over the place,
Some with begging bowls, or
Smeared with ashes, or naked
In the streets. Being holy, being
A devotee of this god or that,
Depending on hand-outs from
The public, is a way of life.

I was told by Vivekananda that
Nalanda came from a favored
Middle-class family. He had
Done well at school and had
Entered the railway service,
Where he had also done well,
Ending up as superintendent
At Bangalore. A faultless
Reputation, a married family
Man; no hint of any instability.
But his whole life was changed

When one night, while taking
A walk in the countryside, he
Met with a celestial messenger.
He knew by the godlike
Aura radiating around the
Old man's head that this
Stranger by the roadside was
Heaven-sent. The ancient
Invited Nalanda to sit on the
Edge of a ditch and said that he
Had flown from Dharamsala
In the Himalayas to instruct
Nalanda, who indeed believed
It because like all Indians he
Believed in parakinesis. He
Knew that servants of the gods,
Like the apsarases, could move
Themselves over thousands of
Miles in the blink of an eye.
They talked together all night.
Then at dawn the messenger
Vanished, but not until he had
Laid on Nalanda the solemn
Injunction to make himself
A serious teacher of Vedanta.
Nalanda was careful to keep
What had happened a secret,
But immediately he began to
Study Vedanta with the wise
Men of the region, giving up
His worldy aspirations, and
He undertook long hours of
Meditation. In a few years he
Was renowned as an adept in
The doctrines of Vedanta and
Their significance, and also as

An eloquent elucidator of the
Ultimate meaning of reality,
Which, as it descends from the
Ancient Vedic texts such as the
Upanishads, concerns especially
The state of being beyond good
And evil, existence beyond and
Above mere knowledge. Then
Sri Nalanda was ready to begin
His teaching, and soon many
Devotees were attracted to him.

On the night of my visit to him
With Professor Vivekananda
The setting for Sri Nalanda's
Lecture was not unlike that of
The Kathakali. It was outdoors
But a tarpaulin extended over
The bathchair in which the sage
Reclined as he talked. He was a
Small man whose somewhat
Birdlike features were belied
By a deep, almost hoarse voice,
More military than priestly.
His head was bald and glinted
As if astrally in the flaring light
Of the brass lanterns. He had
Piercing black eyes. He wore a
White dhoti and sandals. The
Professor and I were seated on
Chairs near him but the others,
The devotees, sat on the ground
In a circle extending out into
The eerie dark. I felt that some
Kind of emanation was coming
From Nalanda into my own

Body, and I'd never had such
An experience before. It was
Not an unpleasant feeling. It
Was more like being a little
High on wine. I couldn't, of
Course, understand what he
Was saying, but Vivekananda
Whispered a word now and then.

I could see I was entirely out of
My depth. I'd had a course or
Two in philosophy at Harvard,
But the abstractions proposed
By Nalanda were from another
Thought-system, one for which
I was ill prepared. I caught bits
Of epistemology, whiffs of the
Philosophy of *Existenz,* but the
Frame was all alien. A different
Kind of mind, a sledgehammer
Of a mind, was at work. I gave
Up trying to understand and let
Myself drift as I watched, lost
In his gestures and intonations.

He lectured for about an hour,
Then rose to give his audience
The namatse blessing, with
Palms together, bowing in a
Circle to include everyone at
The gathering. Then came the
Gifts of food—bread, fruit, and
Vegetables laid out at his feet.
Nalanda asked Vivekananda
And me to stay on. The accent
Of his English was difficult, but

He was cordial, calling me "Mr.
Young America" with a warm
Smile. Vivekananda was well
Versed in Vedanta; they talked
For a half-hour in Malayalam;
And when it was time for us to
Go, Nalanda asked me if I had
A question. But my mind went
Blank: what could I ask of the
Great sage? He smiled and said:
"So, let *me* ask *you* a question.
In America, tell me, what do
They teach you is between two
Thoughts?" I could think of no
Answer to that. I had no answer.
"No matter," said Nalanda. "In
Time you may be ready for such
A question. But fix it in your
Mind. Do not forget it before
You are ready." And all these
Years I've remembered, though
I know I can never answer the
Question. I scarcely understand
It. And is Sri Nalanda still alive?
Wherever he may be, what is
The space between his thoughts?

On my last evening with Raja
Rao we cycled out to the beach
To watch the sunset—a good
One, the sky blazing with many
Colors. At first the setting sun
Seemed a small, distant disk,
But as darkness fell it grew and
Grew into a huge ball of fiery
Red. "That is the great god

Agni," Raja Rao told me, "the
Eternal fire. He is many things.
He is the most important of
The Vedic divinities. First, he
Is the god of the altar fire and
Its sacrifices. Then he is the
Mediator between gods and
Men. And beyond that he is the
God of lightning and the sun."

As we pedaled back through
The dark countryside toward
Trivandrum, we began to smell
The loveliest natural perfume
I've encountered anywhere in
Any country. It's the evening
Scent of India. The people in
Their huts are cooking their
Last meal of the day, using
Cow patties to fuel their fires.
Every patty the cows let fall
Is picked up and saved by the
Children. The smoke rises in
The warm night air softly. It's
A pungent smell and a little
Sweet. It's the smell of India,
Primeval India of the first
Gods and the first real people.

[*The author expresses his thanks to Hayden Carruth for his editorial collaboration on "Trivandrum."*]

INDEX OF TITLES

INDEX OF FIRST LINES

A NOTE ON PUBLICATION

James Laughlin chose the poems for the present volume in the months before his death in November 1997. The poems selected from his earlier books were originally published in the following collections.

Some Natural Things (1945): "The Cave," "Easter in Pittsburgh," "The Last Poem to Be Written," "Mountain Afterglow," "Technical Notes," "What the Pencil Writes."

A Small Book of Poems (1947): "Above the City," "The Sinking Stone," "The Summons."

The Wild Anemone (1957): "In the Museum at Teheran," "Martha Graham," "Near Zermatt: The Drahtseilbahn," "Prognosis," "Rome: In the Café," "Step on His Head," "The Trout," "The Wild Anemone."

In Another Country (1978): "In Another Country," "It Does Me Good," "A Long Night of Dreaming," "Song."

Stolen & Contaminated Poems (1985): "I Hate Love," "In Hac Spe Vivo," "Nothing That's Lovely Can My Love Escape," "To Be Sure," "We Met in a Dream." "What Is It Makes One Girl."

Selected Poems 1935–1985 (1986): "Alba," "The Deconstructed Man," "Elle N'est Pas Noctambule," "The Goddess," "La Gomme à Effacer," "Having Failed," "The House of Light," "Is What We Eat," "J'ignore Où Elle Vague Ce Soir," "The Junk Collector," "A Lady Asks Me," "A Leave-Taking," "La Luciole," "My Old Gray Sweater," "The Old Comedian," "Some of Us Come to Live," "Some People Think," "So Much Depends," "Why," "Will We Ever Go to the Lighthouse?"

The Owl of Minerva (1987): "L'Arrivée du Printemps," "Eyes Are the Guides of Love," "Like the Octopus," "Il Pastor Fido," "Some Memoirs of E.P. (Drafts & Fragments)," "She's Not Exactly Like You," "The Songbird."

The Bird of Endless Time (1989): "The Anginal Equivalent," "At the Boule D'Or," "The Bird of Endless Time," "The Enlacement," "The Happy Poets ['It's my delight to recite']," "Her Letters," "Hic Jacet," "In Half Darkness," "It's March," "Our Bicycles," "Our Meetings," "A

Parable," "The Revenants," "Then and Now," "A Translation," "The Unanswerable Question."

The Man in the Wall (1993): "The Afterthought," "Agatha," "An Attestation," "Before I Die," "The Calves," "A Certain Impermeable Person," "Clutches," "The Flemish Double Portrait," "Long and Languorous," "Making a Love Poem," "The Man in the Wall," "The Shameful Profession," "Silentium Aureatum Est," "The Story of Rhodope," "The Stranger ['There was a knock on the door']," "The Sultan's Justice," "The Thinking Machine," "Time Running Backwards," "The Time Stealer," "La Tristesse," "What the Old Bedouin Told Me."

The Collected Poems of James Laughlin (1994): "Ave Atque Vale," "The Beautiful Muttering," "Building 520, Bellevue," "Dylan," "The Empty Room," "The Eraser," "Eros as Archeologist," "Experience of Blood," "The Firefly," "Having Failed," "I Don't Know Where She Is Wandering Tonight," "The Inn at Kirchstetten," "Into Each Life," "Mon Secret," "The Moths," "My Secret," "O Best of All Nights, Return and Return Again," "With My Third Eye."

Heart Island & Other Epigrams (1995): "At the Post Office," "Les Consolations," "The Consolations," "Elusive Time," "The Gift," "The Happy Poets ['What's happiness?']," "Heart Island," "In Scandinavia," "The Old Man's Lament," "The Two of Them."

The Country Road (1995): "Anima Mea," "The Country Road," "De Contemptu Mortis," "The Departure," "Desert in Bloom," "Do They Make Love?," "A Florilegium," "Her Heart," "How Did Laura Treat Petrach?," "Imprisoned," "The Invisible Room," "Is Memory," "The Mercy in It," "Penelope Venit Abit Helen," "Permanent Memoria," "The Rising Mist at Ard Na Sidhe," "The Search," "A Secret Language," "Some Amatory Epigrams from the Greek Anthology," "Two Fables from *The Ocean of Story*," "When I was a boy with never a crack in my heart," "The Wood Nymph."

The Secret Room (1996): "All Good Things Pass," "All the Clocks," "The Apsarases," "Die Begegnung," "The Calendar Of Fame," "The Crane," "The Darkened Room," "An Elegy of Mimnermus," "The Exquisite Fire," "The Futurist," "The Good of the Sun and Fire," "Good Philosophy," "The Hetaera," "The Honey Bee," "The Immeasurable Boundaries," "The Invitation to Make Love," "I Travel Your Body," "I'm Walking Very Slowly Today," "In Old Age," "In Trivandrum," "The Living Branch," "The Locust," "The Long Feet People,"

"The Magic Flute," "Many Loves," "Moments in Space," "A Night of Ragas," "Penelope to Ulysses," "The Pissing of the Toads," "Poets in Stilts," "The Rescue," "The Right Girl," "The Sculptor," "The Secret Room," "The Secrets," "The Snake Game," "Swapping Minds," "Tanka," "The Tender Letter," "Two for One," "The Unusual Girl," "Word Salad," "The Writer at Work," "The Wrong Bed—Moira," "You're Trouble."